EXPLORING
CHURCH
HISTORY

EXPLORING

CHURCH

HISTORY

James P. Eckman, Ph.D.

CROSSWAY BOOKS • WHEATON, ILLINOIS
A DIVISION OF GOOD NEWS PUBLISHERS

Exploring Church History

Copyright © 2002 by Evangelical Training Association

Published by Crossway Books
    a division of Good News Publishers
    1300 Crescent Street
    Wheaton, Illinois 60187

Previously published by Evangelical Training Association, 1996.

Cover design: Cindy Kiple

First printing 2002

Printed in the United States of America

Scripture quotations are taken from the *New American Standard Bible®* Copyright © The Lockman Foundation 1960, 1962, 1963, 1968, 1971, 1972, 1973, 1975, 1977, 1995. Used by permission. (www.Lockman.org).

Scripture references marked ASV are from the *American Standard Version* of the Bible.

Library of Congress Cataloging-in-Publication Data
Eckman, James P. (James Paul)
    Exploring church history / James P. Eckman.
       p. cm.
    Includes bibliographical references.
    ISBN 1-58134-368-X (pbk. : alk. paper)
    1. Church history. I. Title.
BR145.3 .E25   2002
270—dc21   2001005178
                                   CIP

VP 14 13 12 11 10 09 08 07 06 05
15 14 13 12 11 9 8 7 6 5 4

CONTENTS

INTRODUCTION

In general most Christians are abysmally ignorant of their Christian heritage. Yet an awareness of the history of God's church can help us serve the Lord more effectively. First, knowledge of church history brings a sense of perspective. Many of the cultural and doctrinal battles currently being fought are not really that new. We can gain much from studying the past. Second, church history gives an accurate understanding of the complexities and richness of Christianity. As we realize this diversity and the contributions many individuals and groups have made to the church, it produces a tolerance and appreciation of groups with which we may personally disagree. Finally, church history reinforces the Christian conviction that the church will triumph! Jesus' words, "I will build My church," take on a richer meaning.

As the chapter titles indicate, this book takes a chronological approach to church history—The Ancient Church, The Medieval Church, The Reformation Church, and The Modern Church. Each chapter emphasizes the theological progress and developing consensus within the church on what the Scriptures taught, as well as the institutional development of the church. The chapters on the Reformation (6 and 7) stress the restructuring and fragmentation of the church during the sixteenth and seventeenth centuries. One cannot understand the church today without this background.

Finally, the last five chapters of the book give consideration to the church's struggle with the modern world. Darwinism, Marxism, industrial capitalism, antisupernaturalism, and the challenge of poverty have pressured the church in multiple ways. To a great extent these struggles continue today. Yet through the modern missions movement and revivals, God continues to accomplish His redemptive purposes.

You are about to begin an exciting study. It is my prayer that this book will change your life. I trust that when you are finished, you will have a deeper appreciation for your splendid heritage and a profound conviction that Christ's church will triumph.

ABOUT THE AUTHOR

Dr. James P. Eckman is the Academic Vice-President, Dean, and Professor of Bible and History at Grace University in Omaha, Nebraska. He holds a B.S. from Millersville University of Pennsylvania, an M.A. from Lehigh

University, a Th.M. from Dallas Theological Seminary, and a Ph.D. from the University of Nebraska. While at Dallas Theological Seminary, he received the Charles A. Nash Award in Historical Theology. An ordained minister, Dr. Eckman's specialty is in historical theology, with an emphasis on the American church and revivalism. In addition to hosting a weekly radio program, *Issues in Perspective*, he also performs dramatic monologues on figures from church history such as Augustine, Martin Luther, John Calvin, and Jonathan Edwards. He is married and is the father of two children.

FOUNDATION OF
THE CHURCH:
THE APOSTOLIC AGE

But when the fullness of the time came,
God sent forth His Son . . .

PAUL, THE APOSTLE, GALATIANS 4:4

In Galatians 4:4 the apostle Paul wrote, "But when the fullness of the time came, God sent forth His Son." Paul realized that the first century was a unique period of history, the precise time for God's Son to enter human history.

Unlike any previous period, the Mediterranean world was united. Throughout this world, the imperial armies of Rome maintained a forced peace—the famous *Pax Romana* (30 B.C.–A.D. 180). As the army guarded the empire from robbers and pirates, trade flourished on both land and sea. Prosperity and wealth followed. Rome brought stability and order to its cities, with free food and public games at the taxpayers' expense.

The Roman roads provided an infrastructure that knit the empire together. As a result, the army could be anywhere in the realm within two weeks. Communications from the emperor traveled with a speed unheard of in previous empires. In God's providence, the early church also utilized this communications network to spread the Gospel.

As the imperial army moved with ease through its domain, it carried out the orders of the Caesar with efficiency and discipline. But the

Gospel also penetrated the army. For example, Paul speaks of believers in the Praetorian guard, an elite force closest to the emperor (Phil. 1:13). Also, Christianity first came to Britain through Roman soldiers. So significant was the impact of Christianity on the army that one historian called the Roman army the "mouthpiece of the gospel" (Cairns, 37).

The Roman world was also a Greek world. Rome conquered the Greeks militarily, but in many ways the Greeks conquered Rome intellectually. The common language of the day was *koine* Greek, the language spread throughout the empire by Alexander the Great. In God's sovereignty, this was the language of His revelation, the New Testament. In addition, Greek philosophy heavily influenced the way the Roman world thought. Greek philosophers wanted to know truth and the place of human beings in the universe. Despite the variations within Greek philosophy, most of its philosophers shared the belief that there was a realm beyond the physical world, the domain of the transcendent. Christianity took advantage of this hunger for truth and for transcendent reality. Witness Paul's argument with the philosophers in Acts 17, his presentation of Jesus in Colossians 1, and John's philosophical argument in his Gospel and First Epistle. The Greco-Roman world was intellectually "set up" for the Gospel.

The Roman world also pulsated with religious exhilaration and anticipation. Josephus, a first-century Jewish historian, told of the Eastern cults, false messiahs, and religious fervor that permeated the empire. Many in Israel envisioned the Messiah coming at any moment. The Zealots wanted a revolution against Rome. The Essenes wanted a prophet of light who would expel the darkness of evil. The Pharisees wanted a nationalist leader who would restore the law and free Israel from Rome's oppression.

Furthermore, after the Jewish exile of earlier centuries and the subsequent Diaspora (the migration of Jews throughout the Roman Empire), the synagogue system represented a Jewish presence in every major city. Each time Paul entered a city, he first took the gospel message to the Jews in the synagogue. Only after that did he move on to the Gentiles.

THE LEADERS OF THE APOSTOLIC CHURCH

Peter

Pentecost (fifty days after the crucifixion and ten days after the ascension of Christ) marks the birth of the church. As the Spirit filled the 120 believers who were waiting and praying, the miracle of tongues caused a sensation. Some observers accused the Christians of drunkenness. At this point, Peter emerged as the spokesperson for the early church.

Peter dominates the first fifteen chapters of Acts. As the first among the Twelve to see the resurrected Christ, he emerged as the leader of the small community of believers before Pentecost (Acts 1:15). He even insisted that Judas Iscariot be replaced.

At Pentecost he preached the Spirit-inspired sermon that produced three thousand converts. He cut through the fog of exclusive Judaism by declaring of Jesus that "there is salvation in no one else; for there is no other name under heaven that has been given among men by which we must be saved" (Acts 4:12). He performed miracles, defied the Jerusalem authorities, disciplined Ananias and Sapphira, and set up deacons as helpers so the apostles could study and preach. Despite his slip at Antioch when he withdrew from fellowship with Gentile converts (Gal. 2:14), he championed the Gospel's penetration into the Gentile world.

As the decisive speaker at the Jerusalem Council (A.D. 49) in Acts 15, he brilliantly defended Gentile church membership. After the council, the book of Acts is silent concerning Peter; his activities simply cannot be pinpointed with any certainty. We can, however, be definite about his authorship of 1 and 2 Peter.

Was Peter the founder of the Roman church, its first bishop, and hence its first pope? Incomplete evidence shows he did do missionary work in Antioch and later in Rome, but there is no evidence that he was Rome's bishop or that he stayed long in Rome. In fact, recent scholarship has shown that the church had a presbyterian structure into the second century and was rather decentralized into the fourth. It is difficult to argue that Rome was the ecclesiastical, let alone theological, center of the early Christian church. At best, it was merely a place of honor.

The end of Peter's life is wrapped in tradition. The best evidence establishes that Peter died a martyr's death during Nero's persecutions, about A.D. 68. The apocryphal *Acts of Peter* contends that he died crucified upside down on a Roman cross. That he was crucified would fit Christ's words of John 21:18-19. Of the rest of the tradition, we simply cannot be sure.

John

As one of the "pillars" of the Jerusalem church (Gal. 2:9), John, brother of James and son of Zebedee, was Peter's coworker (Acts 1:13; 3:1–4:23;

8:14-25). Together they healed and preached in the name of Jesus the Messiah. When ordered to stop, they obeyed God rather than men. By laying hands on the new Samaritan converts, Peter and John exercised general supervision over the burgeoning church in Samaria. Although he was probably at the Jerusalem Council of Acts 15, his name does not appear in Acts after his brother James was martyred (Acts 12:1-2). We do not know when he left Jerusalem.

The book of Revelation reveals that John was exiled, probably in the early nineties by Roman Emperor Domitian, to Patmos for preaching the Word of God and for his "testimony of Jesus" (1:9). There John recorded the visions he "saw," which constitute the framework for understanding events surrounding the second coming of Christ. Emperor Nerva apparently released John from exile sometime between A.D. 96 and 98.

After his exile the most reliable evidence places John in Ephesus, where, after living to an old age, he died a natural death. In Ephesus he trained such disciples as Polycarp, Papias, and Ignatius—all strategic leaders of the second-century church. Indeed, this mentoring role may give meaning to his self-described title, "the elder," in 2 and 3 John.

John's most significant contribution to the church was his writing. His Gospel is unique. Only 8 percent of it is related in the synoptic Gospels of Matthew, Mark, and Luke; the remaining 92 percent is original with John. Most exceptional is his instruction regarding the deity of Christ. Jesus is the eternal *Logos* (1:1-18), the great "I am" (8:58).

John likewise gives emphasis to the Spirit, especially in the Upper Room Discourse (14–16). There Jesus asked the Father to send another Helper who will indwell believers, teach them truth and enable them to recall it, and convict the world of its sin, righteousness, and judgment. It is the Spirit who regenerates (3:6), and it is He who brings satisfaction and fulfillment to those who believe in Jesus (7:37-39).

Paul

The other decisive leader of the apostolic church was Paul, in whose life three great ancient traditions intersected. Religiously, he was a Jew, culturally a Greek, and politically a Roman. He was born in Tarsus, a major university town and the principal city of the province of Cilicia. Paul understood his Jewish heritage in terms of the Abrahamic covenant (Phil. 3:5-6). His parents may have named him Saul after Israel's first king, who was also of the tribe of Benjamin. Paul was trained in Pharisaism at the rabbinic school in Jerusalem headed by Gamaliel

(Acts 22:3; Phil. 3:5). His familiarity with Greek authors (Acts 17:28; 1 Cor. 15:33; Titus 1:12) and his use of Greek argumentation (Rom. 2:1–3:20; Col. 1:15-20) suggests a Greco-Roman influence.

The Pharisees were not particularly tolerant of new religious movements. So when the "people of the Way" spread to Damascus (Acts 9:1-2), Rabbi Saul had no problem receiving a commission from the high priest to extradite Jewish Christians to Jerusalem. On the road to that city, Saul met his resurrected Messiah.

Approximately thirteen years separated Paul's conversion and his first missionary journey (A.D. 48). Paul claimed to be *the* missionary to the Gentiles. The missionary journeys that Luke documented in Acts bear this out. The first of these probably provoked the most controversy.

During that trip (Acts 13–14), Paul and Barnabas evangelized Cyprus and the southern part of Galatia. As Gentile churches flourished, two fundamental questions surfaced: What was the relationship between Christianity and Judaism? How is a person justified? A Judaistic group from Judea insisted that circumcision was necessary for salvation—something that contradicted Paul's free-grace Gospel. Hence the Jerusalem Council of Acts 15.

The council affirmed Paul's doctrine of free grace, adding only that Gentile converts abstain from certain practices. Thus the mother church affirmed Paul's ministry of justification by faith plus nothing! Following the council, Paul embarked on two additional missionary journeys that are recorded in Acts 15:26–21:16.

After these journeys he went to Jerusalem to report to James and the elders about his activities in the Gentile churches. There, as a result of trumped-up charges, Roman authorities arrested him. Over the next two years, Paul was imprisoned in Caesarea and stood trial before the Roman procurator Felix, his successor Porcius Festus, and Herod Agrippa II, the titular king of the Jews. Asserting his Roman citizenship, he appealed to Caesar and headed for Rome where officials placed him under house arrest.

Because of the difficulty of determining the exact chronology and place names that appear in the Pastoral Epistles (1 and 2 Timothy and Titus), it seems best to assume that Paul was subsequently released and ministered for six more years (A.D. 62–67). Some scholars even suggest that Paul not only ministered to Asia Minor and Greece but also reached Spain before he was arrested at the height of Nero's persecutions. He was most likely executed by decapitation in the spring of A.D. 68.

SIGNIFICANT WOMEN OF THE NEW TESTAMENT

The Scriptures affirm the equality of men and women, both created in the image of God (Gen. 1:26-27) and in their position in Christ (Gal. 3:28). While the Bible proclaims equality of the sexes, it also argues for functional differences (role differences) within the home (Eph. 5:22-33; Col. 3:18-19) and within the church (1 Cor. 11:2-16; 14:33-36; 1 Tim. 2:8-15; 3:1-13; 5:1-25; Titus 1:6-9). Whatever the precise meanings and applications of these crucial Pauline passages may be, church history bears witness to an extraordinary number of women in the early church.

The Gospel was a liberating force in the ancient world, challenging old and established traditions rooted in human prejudice. These gradually died. Contempt, discrimination, and demeaning references often characterized rabbinic teachings about women. Rabbis, for instance, were encouraged not to teach women or even speak to them. According to Jewish tradition, women could never be a part of the count needed to establish a synagogue. But Luke cited both men and women who were baptized and persecuted and who contributed to the growth of the church (Acts 5:14; 8:12; 9:2; 17:4, 12).

Women in Jesus' Day

The challenge to ancient traditions began with Jesus' earthly ministry, in which women played a most significant role. Many women financially supported the ministry of Jesus and His disciples and ministered to Him personally (Matt. 27:55-56; Mark 15:40-41; Luke 8:3). The Gospels usually depict Mary, sister of Martha, as seated at Jesus' feet—an honor normally given to men. Several women had the immensely important distinction of bearing the news of Christ's resurrection—a quite remarkable honor in light of strict Jewish teachings on valid testimony.

Not only were women involved in the ministry of Jesus, but they participated in the events at Pentecost (Acts 1:14). Since the narrative of events in the Upper Room continues into Acts 2, we must assume that the women present were likewise filled with the Holy Spirit at Pentecost (2:1-4).

Women in the Early Church

The book of Acts also gives accounts of women who played active roles in ministry in the early church. Dorcas (Tabitha) was the only woman in the New Testament to be called a "disciple" (9:36). Her death caused a major stir in Joppa, prompting the believers to urge Peter to travel from nearby Lydda. Peter prayed, and Dorcas was raised from the dead!

Mary of Jerusalem, John Mark's mother (12:12), was a wealthy widow whose house became the vital hub of the Jerusalem church. There the young church found refuge and security during the intense persecutions of Herod Agrippa. Lydia, a wealthy woman of commerce and apparently Paul's first convert in Europe, opened her home to Paul and Silas (16:14-15).

But the early church did not limit women to nonverbal ministry. One of the more remarkable women of the New Testament was Priscilla (Prisca). She and her husband, Aquila, early converts to the faith, were banished from Rome. They became intimate friends with Paul, with whom they shared hospitality and the craft of tent-making (Acts 18:1-3). In some way they had risked their lives for Paul (Rom. 16:3-5), perhaps at the same time heightening his awareness of the growing church in Rome. Most significantly, both Priscilla and Aquila took Apollos, the eloquent preacher from Alexandria, "and explained to him the way of God more accurately" (Acts 18:26). Obviously Priscilla knew biblical truth and could explain it with clarity. That the ministry of this couple was well known and widespread is evidenced by the frequent references to them in Paul's writings (Rom. 16:3; 1 Cor. 16.19, 2 Tim. 4:19). Tradition has it that Priscilla was martyred in Rome.

Another woman of New Testament significance was Phoebe (Rom. 16:1-2). Because she was probably the bearer of Paul's letter to the Romans, Paul commends her to the Roman church, asking that they "receive her in the Lord in a manner worthy of the saints," and "help her in whatever matter she may have need of you." He also says of her that she was a "helper," which clearly implies active and important functions in the church. Was she, therefore, representing Paul in some official capacity, as perhaps a "deaconess" ("servant" of v. 1), as some have argued? From these two verses, we simply cannot be certain she held an authoritative office in the church at Cenchrea. However, it is clear that Phoebe was significant enough for Paul to go out of his way to single her out and ask the Roman church to take care of her.

Two passages indicate that women functioned as prophets in the early church. Acts 21:9 introduces Philip the evangelist as having four daughters who were "prophetesses." From Paul's instruction in 1 Corinthians 11:5, it would seem that Philip's daughters were not exceptions, for Paul's instructions about women's head coverings occurs in the context of women "praying or prophesying" in the worship service. Whatever the nature of these ministries, women gifted by the Holy Spirit exercised notable responsibilities in the early church.

Other women of the New Testament fulfilled pivotal ministry roles. Euodias and Syntyche (Phil. 4:2-3) were identified as "fellow workers" with Paul, a remarkable designation when one remembers that Paul also labeled Titus and Timothy "fellow workers." Paul classified Andronicus and Junias [Junia] (Rom. 16:7)—probably a husband and wife—as "outstanding among the apostles," most likely a reference to their role as ones commissioned by the Roman church for special duties, not the New Testament office of apostle. Finally, in the list of "fellow workers" in Romans 16, ten of the twenty-nine people commended by Paul were women.

Women thus played a decisive role in the beginning of Christianity. Their work both complemented the duties of men and involved some leadership responsibilities. Although there are no recorded examples of women evangelists, elders, or formal teachers of biblical truth, their function was both vibrant and vital in the ongoing progress of the Gospel—a clear testimony to the liberating power of Jesus Christ.

With the deaths of Peter, Paul, and John, the mantle of leadership passed to a new generation, the Apostolic Fathers. The Fathers stood on the shoulders of giants, but their theology was often undeveloped. We take up their story in the next chapter.

FOR FURTHER DISCUSSION

1. What was the Pax Romana, and what were some of its characteristics?
2. How did the great Roman road system aid the spread of the Gospel?
3. What were some of the important contributions that Greek philosophy made to the setting of the Roman world?
4. Who were some of the groups of first-century Judaism, and what were their expectations?
5. List some of the decisive contributions that Peter, Paul, and John each made to the apostolic church.
6. In what roles were women involved in the early church, according to the New Testament?

2

TIIE APOSTOLIC FATHERS

The test of one's doctrine is following the bishop.
The Episcopal office comes from God, not from man.
Christians are to respect him as they
respect God the Father.

IGNATIUS OF ANIIOCH,

EPISTLE TO THE EPHESIANS

By the end of the first century, the death of the apostles produced a leadership vacuum in the church. Who had the authority to lead the believers? Who would guide and guard this flourishing new Christian faith? A group generally called the Church Fathers filled the gap.

As a term of affection and esteem, "father" was generally given to spiritual leaders of the church (known as elders or bishops). The Fathers can be divided into three groups: the Apostolic Fathers (A.D. 95–150), the Apologists (A.D. 150–300), and the Theologians (A.D. 300–600). The Apostolic Fathers wrote what was generally devotional and edifying in nature; the Apologists produced literature that defended the faith and countered error; the Theologians began doing systematic theology. The next several chapters cover each of these groups.

This chapter concentrates on the Apostolic Fathers, individuals who wrote Christian literature and gave leadership to the church from A.D. 95 to 150. Their writings reflected a deep commitment to the Old Testament and an understanding that the new faith of Christianity fulfilled the Old Testament. There is, therefore, little theological reflection or doctrinal analysis from the Apostolic Fathers. Their desire was to edify and exhort the saints and give them the hope they needed to persevere. We can best describe their work as devotional, pietistic (encouraging holy living), and pastoral.

The Apostolic Fathers served and led a church exploding with growth and zeal. Such realities demanded counsel, advice, and practical guidelines for spiritual growth and action for both individual Christians and local church bodies. Thus the writings of the Apostolic Fathers often glorified martyrdom and celibacy and stressed the importance of baptism in ways that make modern evangelicals quite uncomfortable. But the time in which they wrote, the first fifty years of the second century, marked a church struggling with how to live obediently and how to structure the church in a vastly pagan culture.

Clement of Rome

As the bishop, or elder, of Rome, Clement (A.D. 30–100) shouldered the responsibility for dealing with a major disturbance in Corinth. As when Paul wrote to the church forty years earlier, the Corinthian church suffered from factionalism and bitterness. Therefore, Clement exhorted the Corinthians to exercise love, patience, and humility as the key to develop sound Christian interpersonal relationships. He also underscored obedience to church leadership as essential for church harmony and desperately needed unity.

Because it is the earliest example of Christian literature outside the New Testament, Clement's letter to the Corinthians is profoundly important. He quoted the Old Testament so frequently that we can readily see how dependent the early church was on its authority. His many allusions to Paul's writings and life also show how widespread Paul's influence was. Finally, as Clement called for obedience to the church leadership, he argued that church elders received their authority from the apostles, who received their authority from Christ. Over the next several centuries, the church decisively expanded this idea of succession.

Ignatius

Because of his martyrdom, Ignatius is considered a giant among the early Church Fathers. The bishop of Antioch in Syria, he was arrested by Roman authorities for his Christian testimony. As he made his way to Rome for execution, he visited several cities along the way. His subsequent letters to these seven churches, written about A.D. 110, stressed the twin themes of heresy and unity. The heresy he addressed was an early form of Gnostic teaching (see the next chapter), which denied the full humanity of Jesus. Thus Ignatius argued that the best defense against such heresy and the foremost guarantee of unity was the bishop.

When Ignatius called for submission to the bishop, he revealed a subtle change developing in the early church. The New Testament documents show a plurality of church leadership in the first century, principally elders and deacons. However, the growth of the church in the empire demanded a greater degree of authority and superintendence over the local churches. That is apparently why Ignatius stressed to the elders and deacons of the seven churches that they submit to a bishop who would coordinate and rule over their local churches. This, he claimed, was necessary to deal with false teaching and to foster unity among the churches. Subsequent generations of church leaders expanded the office of bishop.

The Shepherd of Hermas

Written about A.D. 150 by a freed slave, The Shepherd of Hermas is a rather bizarre work of five visions patterned somewhat after John's book of the Revelation. In graphic detail, Hermas, drawing on personal experiences of himself and his family, depicted the evils of a decadent civilization very much in decline. Repentance and the call to holy living dominate the work.

Polycarp

As a disciple of the apostle John and as bishop of Smyrna, Polycarp wrote a most significant letter to the church at Philippi about A.D. 110. The value of this letter with its copious Old Testament quotations is its dependence on many of the circulating books of the New Testament, especially those written by Paul. This letter shows that the early second-century church regarded the New Testament books as authoritative in calling Christians to holy living.

Polycarp's martyrdom at age eighty-six in A.D. 155 remains one of the great narratives of the early church. At his trial he did nothing to provoke his accusers but passionately defended Jesus Christ as his Lord. He died at the fiery stake, giving praise to his Lord. Venerated for centuries as a model martyr, Polycarp illustrates the truth stated by the apologist Tertullian later that "the blood of martyrs is the seed of the church."

Didache

One of the most significant of the early church writings is the Didache, or The Teaching of the Twelve. Probably written during the first decade of the second century as a church manual, the Didache presents a remarkable picture of early church life. The manual gives counsel on how to do baptisms, how to conduct worship services and the Lord's Table, and how to exercise church discipline. The book likewise furnishes valuable advice on how to detect false teaching in the church. The final part of the manual exhorts Christians to holy living in light of the second coming of Jesus.

Other writings of the Apostolic Fathers survive, and each reflects the themes summarized in this chapter. However, in about A.D. 150 a significant change occurs in the writings of the church leaders. One notes a more apologetic style as the leaders combat theological error creeping into the church. This shift marks the beginning of the second group of Church Fathers known as the Apologists, the subject of the next chapter.

FOR FURTHER DISCUSSION

1. Summarize the reasons why the church used the term "father" when referring to their early leaders.
2. What are the three major chronological periods of the Church Fathers?
3. List three characteristics of the writings of the Apostolic Fathers.
4. Who did Ignatius say was the best defense against heresy and the greatest promoter of unity? Why did he say that?

3

DEFENDING THE FAITH: ENEMIES WITHIN AND WITHOUT

The blood of the martyrs is the seed of the church.

TERTULLIAN

Defending Christian truth has always been of foremost importance in church history. As the church moved into the late second century, this need was especially acute, for both inside and outside the church false teaching and error abounded. Thus God raised up a group of individuals—the Apologists—who defended the Christian faith and, in doing so, led the church toward deeper theological truth. Error forced the church to think more precisely about what it believed and to reach a consensus on what the Scriptures taught.

Most of the error was a crude mixture of Greek philosophy, Judaism, and other Eastern beliefs that assailed Christian teaching about Jesus Christ and His work. Nonbelievers often characterized Christians as atheists, cannibals, or immoral people. The first criticism arose because Christians refused to worship the emperor or the Greco-Roman gods. The second accusation resulted from a misconception about the Lord's Supper and the third from a misunderstanding of the love displayed within the early church.

HERESIES OUTSIDE THE CHURCH

Gnosticism

No other heresy threatened early Christianity more than Gnosticism. Reaching its height in the second century, Gnosticism had its origins at least a century earlier. At its center, this philosophy has a dualistic view of reality. The material world and the immaterial world were totally separate, the material being intrinsically evil and the immaterial being intrinsically good. For the Gnostics, it was inconceivable that a good God could have created such an evil, material world. Thus they argued that a divine spark, or emanation, from God created the physical universe. It was equally difficult for the Gnostics to believe that Jesus could have had a physical body. Many Gnostics argued Jesus only "appeared" to have a physical body.

These teachings were part of a special body of knowledge, or *gnosis*, that was necessary for salvation. This special knowledge God imparted only to an elite few. Because the soul alone was good, salvation was purely spiritual; there was no place for the resurrection of the body in Gnosticism. The very heart of Christianity was at stake!

Manichaeism

A bizarre cousin to Gnosticism, Manichaeism also was rooted in dualism. Following the teachings of Mani (216–276), this philosophy proclaimed that two opposing forces, light and darkness, were in eternal combat. Salvation was achieved by the children of light through a life of self-denial and celibacy.

Neoplatonism

Built on the teachings of Plato, this highly mystical challenge to Christianity taught that the goal of all humans was reabsorption into the divine essence. Reabsorption was accomplished through various processes including meditation, contemplation, and other mystical disciplines. Salvation was purely spiritual with no Jesus, no cross, and no atonement.

ERRORS WITHIN THE CHURCH

Marcionism

Marcion was a second-century heretic who established a vibrant rival church in Rome. He argued that there were two gods—a creator and a redeemer. The former was the god of the Old Testament, who was evil and capricious. The latter was the god of love and redemption, whom Jesus Christ revealed.

Because of his view of God, Marcion also developed his own canon of Scripture. He totally rejected the Old Testament for its portrayal of God. He likewise repudiated major segments of the New Testament, accepting only portions of Luke's Gospel and only ten Epistles of Paul. Marcion thought that all the other books betrayed a Judaistic, Old Testament bias.

This man's ideas were poison to the early church. As a person of wealth and influence, he used both to establish a rival church in Rome that actually lasted for several centuries. In God's sovereignty, Marcion's influence was positive; he forced the church to think more carefully and systematically about the nature of the Godhead and about the canon of Scripture.

Ebionitism

This strange movement emerged late in the first century and continued into the fourth. In many ways, Ebionitism resembled the false teaching with which Paul did battle in the book of Galatians. Ebionites taught that Jesus was the prophetic successor to Moses—not the eternal second person of the Trinity. Furthermore, the Ebionites were legalists who viewed Jesus as an exalted man who perfectly kept the law. Coming from their dualism, they were ascetics, practicing a life of poverty, self-denial, and often elaborate rituals. Legalistic to the core, Ebionites challenged the free-grace Gospel of Christianity.

Montanism

Started by Montanus, this movement had its center in Phrygia (modern Turkey) in the second century. Central to Montanus was the revelation—the "New Prophecy"—that the coming of Christ was near. Obedience to the Paraclete (the Holy Spirit) through His messenger—Montanus—was the standard. Necessarily, the movement involved use of the sign gifts as evidence of anointing for the Second Coming. The movement also advocated a rigid asceticism that included celibacy and prolonged fasting. The Montanists challenged the authority of church officials and stood outside the developing New Testament canon. For these reasons, the church condemned the Montanists. The contribution of the movement was that it forced the church to think more precisely about the Holy Spirit's role in Christianity.

EMPIRE PERSECUTIONS

For the first few decades of the church, the Roman Empire regarded Christianity as a sect of Judaism and largely left it alone. However, with the growth of the church, this policy changed. Caesar Nero ruthlessly persecuted Christians in the late 60s. But the first empire-wide persecutions did not occur until the reign of Decius in 250, who attempted to enforce sacrifices to the Roman gods.

The most merciless persecutions occurred under Emperor Diocletian in the early 300s. He ordered the destruction of church buildings, the burning of the Scriptures, the closing of church meetings, and the imprisonment of Christians. Later he made the refusal to sacrifice to the gods a capital crime.

Increased persecution forced the church to determine what was really important. For what were church members willing to die? For what holy writings were members willing to die? The Apologists sought to determine the answers to these questions.

MAJOR APOLOGISTS AND THEIR WRITINGS

Justin Martyr

Justin was born about 100 in the biblical town of Shechem in Samaria. Extremely well educated for his day, Justin dabbled in all the popular philosophies—those of the Stoics, Plato, and Aristotle. He even committed himself for a while to the philosophy of the mathematician Pythagoras.

But, as he explained in his book *Dialogue with Trypho*, his search for truth ended when, while walking along the seashore near Ephesus, he met an elderly Christian who steered him toward the Scriptures. The correspondence between Old Testament prophecies and their fulfillment in Jesus Christ impressed him. At the age of thirty-three, he embraced the Christian faith.

He continued to pursue philosophical truth, but this time through the grid of the revealed truth of Scripture. Although he founded a Christian school in Rome, his ministry was largely an itinerant one of presenting the superior philosophical position of Christianity. It alone could bring the balanced and noble life that the ancients had sought in Greek philosophy.

Through this ministry, he gathered many disciples, among them Tatian, another famous Apologist. He also battled Marcion. Justin condemned Marcion's view of God as heretical and defended the Old Testament as God's Word. As he demonstrated the continuity of the two Testaments, Justin quoted or alluded to all four Gospels, Acts, eight of Paul's epistles, and 1 Peter. His defense of the integrity of God's Word was crucial to the developing conviction of the New Testament's authority.

However, Justin's greatest legacy was his writing. He wrote two

Apologies and the penetrating *Dialogue with Trypho*. The two *Apologies* were directed to the Roman government and offered a brilliant defense of Christianity as far superior to any of the pagan religions or philosophies. He likewise targeted what he saw as the thoroughly unjust persecution of Christians.

His *Dialogue with Trypho* is essentially the narration of a conversation between Justin and Trypho, an educated Jew who was immersed in Greek philosophy. Quite central to the book is Justin's obvious passion to convince Jews that Jesus was the prophesied Old Testament Messiah. At the end of the book, Justin eloquently appealed to Trypho to accept the truth about Jesus and the Christian faith.

Like most of the early church leaders, Justin's theology was not well developed. He believed in the Trinity and the deity of Jesus, but he did not work out the complexities of the Godhead or the relationship between the deity and the humanity of Jesus. His background in Greek philosophy was often more of a hindrance than a help.

During a trip to Rome, about 165, Justin and six other Christians were arrested. After a mock trial in which they refused to recant their faith, they were all beheaded—hence the name, Justin Martyr.

Irenaeus

Irenaeus was one of the earliest and most distinguished opponents of Gnosticism. He was born in Asia Minor around 135. There he knew and was apparently influenced by Polycarp. Irenaeus may have been one of the early missionaries to Gaul (modern France), for by 177 he was the recognized bishop of Lyons. There he spent his life pastoring, teaching, commissioning missionaries to the rest of Europe, and writing. He was evidently martyred about 202.

Two major works of Irenaeus survive: *The Demonstration of the Apostolic Preaching* and *Against Heresies*. The first work detailed the Christian faith proved from Scripture and called for readers to defend proper doctrine against heresy. The second work clearly targeted the Gnostics. From his writing we can conclude much about the developing theology of the second-century church.

First, he was the earliest of the Apologists to have a fully developed view of scriptural authority. His arguments refer to both Testaments; in fact, he quoted or alluded to all but four of the New Testament books. He also saw great continuity between the two Testaments, presenting Jesus as the fulfiller of Old Testament prophecies.

Second, because the Gnostics had such a distorted view of Jesus,

Irenaeus considered Jesus Christ the very core of theology. Christ was the basis for the continuity between creation and redemption. What humanity lost in Adam is regained in Christ. In attacking Gnostic dualism, Irenaeus also argued for the literal nature of Jesus' physical body and the absolute centrality of the resurrection of the physical body.

Third, despite his orthodox positions on many central issues of theology, his beliefs held seeds of error that would later flower in medieval Catholicism. For example, in dealing with the Gnostics, he emphasized the physical presence of Christ in the bread and cup—an early form of transubstantiation. Also, his choice of words when it came to the ordinance of baptism seem to indicate that forgiveness accompanied the ordinance. Finally, as he contrasted Adam and Christ, he gave a special place to Mary, Jesus' mother, as the "new Eve." He taught that her obedience made possible the restoration of humanity. Such teaching was evidence of the developing veneration of Mary that would characterize mature Roman Catholicism.

Origen

Thoroughly committed to the inspiration and authority of Scripture, Origen wrote the first real systematic theology in church history as well as numerous commentaries on books of the Bible. He was born and lived part of his life in Alexandria, Egypt, one of the important intellectual and theological centers of the early church. After finishing his studies, he became head of the Catechetical School at Alexandria, a position he held for twenty-eight years. Due to a struggle with the Alexandrian bishop, Origen ended up in Caesarea where he ministered for the remaining twenty years of his life. He suffered intense torture during the Roman persecutions and died around 254.

Because Origen wanted the church to combat the growing heresies, he committed himself to making the tools for Bible study available. Most significant was his extraordinary work called the *Hexapla*, an edition of the Old Testament including the Hebrew text, the Greek transliteration of the Hebrew text, and four available Greek translations in six parallel columns. A monumental work that took twenty-eight years to complete, it enabled Christians to study the Old Testament with all available scholarship in one book. It also verified the accuracy of the Septuagint, the major Greek translation of the Old Testament.

Origen's interpretation of the sacred text got him in trouble. He taught that allegory was the key to unlock the mysteries of the text, and it was up to the interpreter to find the allegorical key. The centrality of

Christ in Scripture gave his method its dynamic. For example, when it came to the Levitical laws and ceremonies, literalness did not help, he argued. Only allegory aided the interpreter in seeing Jesus in the Levitical system.

His championing of the allegorical method profoundly influenced scriptural interpretation for hundreds of years. Yet the influence of allegorical interpretation has been largely negative. Who is to decide if the proper hidden meaning has been found? What is the standard? As a tool for interpretation, allegory is simply too subjective.

Origen's zeal to serve the Lord also resulted in a deep devotion to asceticism—a life of self-denial—and greatly impacted the monastic communities of later centuries. In his commentary on the Song of Solomon, he stressed that material things and even other people can hinder a person from attaining the deeper spiritual life. Therefore, he denied himself adequate sleep, fasted, and walked barefoot.

The Apologists made their mark in church history as they contended for the faith and began to systematize theological truth. Through their work the church reached consensus on the twenty-seven books of the New Testament canon. The church also inaugurated its ecclesiastical structure, with the office of bishop becoming more significant. Most importantly, the Apologists laid the foundation for the mature theological reflection that characterized the Theologians, the topic of our next chapter.

FOR FURTHER DISCUSSION

1. Summarize Gnostic and Manichaean dualism. What does it mean? Why is it incorrect?
2. Explain why the Gnostic view of Jesus was wrong.
3. In what ways are Gnosticism, Manichaeism, and Neoplatonism similar?
4. What was the Ebionite view of Jesus?
5. Why was Marcion a threat to Christian beliefs about the Bible?
6. Where was the error of Montanism?
7. Summarize Justin's contribution as an Apologist.

The Apologists

Who?	Major Writings?	Main Focus?
Justin Martyr (circa A.D. 100–165)	*Two Apologies, Dialogue with Trypho*	Defense of authority of the Old and New Testaments
Irenaeus (circa A.D. 135–202)	*The Demonstration of Apostolic Preaching, Against Heresies*	Attacked the dualism of the Gnostics by defending the centrality of the physical resurrection of Jesus
Origen (circa A.D. 185–254)	*Hexapla*	Developed tools for Bible study

THE ANCIENT CHURCH
AND THEOLOGY

O God! Our souls find no rest until they rest in you.

AUGUSTINE

About the year 300, the winds of theological change were blowing through the church. Theological disputes over the nature of the Godhead, the nature of Jesus, and the doctrine of salvation caused the church to systematize its beliefs and reach consensus on what the Scriptures taught. Spiritual giants such as Athanasius and Augustine dominated this period and solidified the theology of Christianity. This period is profoundly important for our understanding of church history.

THE PREINCARNATE NATURE OF JESUS CHRIST

Controversy erupted in the early 300s over the teachings of a North African priest named Arius. Influenced by Greek rationalism, Arius argued for an absolute monotheism that denied the deity of Jesus and claimed that He was a created being. Similar to modern Jehovah's Witnesses, Arius contended that "there was a time when he was not" (Kelly, 228). Jesus was, therefore, of a different essence than the Father. Arius's commitment to Greek thought demanded that God, who is spirit and absolutely indivisible, could never truly identify with humanity, which is basically material. The two were forever irreconcilable. Thus only a creature, created within time, could possibly bridge that gap. That creature was Jesus Christ.

The Roman Emperor Constantine, himself a Christian who had ended the persecution of the church in A.D. 313, called the Council of Nicea in 325 to deal with the uproar. Three positions were represented at Nicea: 1) Jesus was of a *different* essence from the Father (Arius); 2) Jesus was of the *same* essence as the Father (Athanasius); 3) Jesus was of a *like* essence to the Father (a compromise position).

The debate was heated and often bitter. But the creed that Nicea produced forthrightly condemned Arius as a heretic. Arguing that Jesus was of the *same* essence as the Father, the Nicene Creed declared Jesus to be "true God from true God" (Leith, 30). And denying one of the central tenets of Arianism, the council proclaimed Jesus as "begotten, not created" (Leith, 31).

Arius's arch opponent was Alexander, bishop of Alexandria, whose personal secretary was Athanasius. Athanasius played a small but important role at Nicea. But for the next forty-five years, he defended the Nicene formula. He taught that the members of the Trinity are coequal, coessential, and coeternal. He powerfully linked the doctrines of the Trinity and salvation. From Scripture he argued that God created humanity in His image, but through sin, humanity abandoned Him and His image. Thus a new creation was necessary, and only God could be the Savior of fallen humanity. No man could possibly provide this needed redemption. For Athanasius, then, the deity of Jesus Christ and the salvation of fallen humanity were inextricably linked. This Apologist was willing to suffer any punishment or persecution to defend that crucial bond, for to deny the deity of Jesus was to emasculate the Gospel.

THE THREE CAPPADOCIANS—DEFENDING THE TRINITY

One of the most profound truths of the Christian faith is the doctrine of the Trinity. It separates Christianity from all other world religions.

The Bible teaches in Deuteronomy 6:4 that God is one; yet from the New Testament it is clear that this one God consists of three persons— Father, Son, and Holy Spirit. The church has always affirmed this doctrine as orthodox, but wrestling with its theological and philosophical implications has been difficult. Especially in the early church, this struggle often produced heresy.

The ancient church of the third and fourth centuries was plagued with false teaching that challenged the deity of Jesus and the Holy Spirit. Whether it was the teachings of Arius or a group called the Pneumatomachians, the Son and the Spirit were regarded as subordinate to the Father. In order to preserve the oneness of God, others argued that Jesus was a man who was adopted as the Son of God; thus He was not eternally the Son.

Others contended that there was one God who revealed Himself in one of three modes—Father, Son, or Spirit. To decide the issue, the early church asked, "Is this what the Scriptures teach?" More specifically, what precise, descriptive words could guard against heresy when it comes to explaining the relationship between the Father, Son, and Spirit? Even into the fifth century, the church labored over these questions.

The orthodox doctrine of the Trinity was a product of a series of debates and councils, sparked in large part by heretical teaching from within the church. It was the collaboration of three friends, the Three Cappadocians—Basil of Caesarea (circa 330-379), Gregory of Nazianzus (circa 329-389), and Gregory of Nyssa (circa 330-394)—that produced the victory over many of these heresies. God clearly used them in a mighty way to formulate the truth about the relationship between the members of the Godhead. Until modern religious liberalism emerged in the nineteenth century, their work provided the definitive framework for thinking and speaking about the Trinitarian God we worship.

Brief biographical sketches place all three as key leaders in the Eastern church. Basil was born into a wealthy Christian family in what would be modern Turkey. Well educated in the schools of Greece, he was appointed bishop of Caesarea. His influence in the development of monasticism was enormous.

His brother, Gregory of Nyssa, became a teacher of rhetoric and was appointed bishop of Nyssa. While the Arians were in resurgence in the Eastern empire, he was deposed and sent into exile for five years. Their mutual friend, Gregory of Nazianzus, was also educated at the universities at Alexandria and Athens, where he met Basil. To one degree or another, each was philosophical, mystical, and monastic. But they shared a deep commitment to orthodox Nicene Christianity. Passionately, each defended the members of the Trinity as coequal, coessential, and coeternal.

Perhaps Basil made the most significant contribution in championing the orthodox view of the Trinity. The language used by theologians of the early church often depicted the Son as subordinate to the Father; He was thus in some way inferior. When it came to the Holy Spirit, there was very little discussion at all.

Basil showed that when we think of the Trinitarian God, we must always separate the terms "essence" and "person"; they are not synonyms. "Essence" is what makes God, God. Attributes such as omnipotence, omnipresence, and omniscience are involved here. "Person" is a term that defines the distinctions within that one essence. Thus we can correctly say "God the Father," "God the Son," and "God the Spirit," while maintaining that they are one and inseparable in being. Basil was also the first theologian to write a major treatise on the Holy Spirit in which he offered proofs for the deity of the Spirit.

Gregory of Nazianzus took the argument a step further. Agreeing with his friend Basil's contention of the difference between essence and person, Gregory showed that the difference between the three persons is relational. This relationship is delineated as eternally the Father, eternally the Son, and eternally the Spirit. Eternally there has been love and communion between the persons of one essence that constitute the Trinity.

Basil's brother, Gregory of Nyssa, also showed that the difference between the members of the Godhead is not one of essence or of substance. The difference can be grounded only on the inner relations and functions of each. Any language that results in the Son's being subordinate to the Father or of the Spirit's being subordinate to the Son is simply unacceptable.

Thus the Trinity is one God of three persons whose difference is relational and functional, not essential. We do not have three gods or three modes of God; we have one God. Ephesians 1:1-14 illustrates the point quite well—the Father chooses, the Son redeems, the Spirit seals (see also 2 Cor. 13:14; 1 Pet. 1:2). Each member of the Godhead is intimately involved in the drama of salvation. We thus can follow Paul and praise the Trinitarian God of grace!

It is difficult for us in the modern church to imagine how much the early church struggled with choosing the proper words when discussing the nature of the Godhead. But in each generation God raised up individuals to protect the church from error. The Three Cappadocians teach us the importance of precise thinking when it comes to the Trinity. Their precision won the day at the Council of Constantinople in 381 where the forces of heretical thinking were defeated.

DEFINING THE DOCTRINE OF THE GOD-MAN

The touchstone of theological orthodoxy is the person of Christ. Both His deity and His humanity must be affirmed, or the entire doctrine of salvation is affected. Only a Jesus who is truly God and truly man can provide a complete salvation for humanity.

A problem in the early church was explaining how Jesus' deity and His humanity related. At any given point in His earthly life, how did His two natures blend? Was He more God or more man? How should we view the union of these two natures in the one person? The debate over Jesus' two natures troubled the church for more than 300 years, at least until 451 at the Council of Chalcedon, when the definitive statement about Jesus' two natures was written.

As one studies the early church, it becomes clear that the emergence of error usually prompted the church to seek a more satisfactory explanation of a theological question. This was true of the doctrine of Christ. Throughout the period from 325 to 451, major interpretations emerged, often heretical, that challenged the church to think more precisely about defining the relationship of Jesus' two natures.

The Alexandrian School

Two schools of theology, one in Antioch and the other in Alexandria, Egypt, framed the debate on the nature of Christ. The Alexandrian school claimed such luminaries as Athanasius and the great Origen. Influenced by Greek philosophy, especially Plato, the Alexandrians tended to elevate the spiritual—Christ's deity—at the expense of His humanity.

Following logically from the Alexandrian position came the heresy propagated by Apollinarius. He was a friend of Athanasius and Basil the Great as well as a teacher of the great Jerome. However, he taught that Jesus was fully God but that His "rational soul" was supplanted by the divine *Logos*. This meant that Jesus was not completely human.

The Council of Constantinople in 381 condemned Apollinarius as a heretic because his view affected the doctrine of salvation. How could Christ sufficiently die for humans if He was not totally a man Himself? The council thus concluded that Jesus had to be completely human and completely divine.

The Antiochene School

The second major school of theology, in Antioch, was influenced by Aristotle, who saw man as a unity of soul and body, not a dichotomy. This school gave far more importance to the unique distinction of Jesus' two natures than did the Alexandrians. The Antiochene emphasis logically produced the heresy Nestorianism, named after Nestorius, who further challenged the church's thinking about Jesus.

As Patriarch in Constantinople in 428, Nestorius held a powerful position in the early church. For several reasons he was uncomfortable with the way the Alexandrians were using certain phrases about Jesus, all of which he thought amounted to a dangerous mixing of the human and divine natures of Christ. His solution was to maintain an absolute distinction of the two natures to such an extent that the only connection between them was the will.

The best analogy of how Nestorius viewed Christ was as a Siamese twin. Because the patriarch could not imagine deity being involved in human suffering or change, he insisted that the two natures were artificially joined. Even though some modern scholarship doubts whether Nestorius actually taught this, this teaching was condemned as heresy at the Council of Ephesus in 431.

It was clear that neither the rigid two-nature model of Nestorius nor the careless one-nature theory of Apollinarius corresponded with the biblical data. In Jesus' confrontation with the Samaritan woman at the well in John 4, His two natures seemed to be in perfect communion. At any given moment in time, He was both God and man. Thus a position was needed that would combine the strength of both proposals.

A monk from Constantinople named Eutyches proposed a model for understanding Christ that attempted to reconcile Apollinarius and Nestorius. He refused to maintain a clear distinction between the two natures of Jesus; instead, he argued for a mixture of the natures such that a third confused mingling was the result. The analogy of dropping a few drops of oil into a pail of water illustrates the point—both the oil and the water are present, but the distinction between the two is not clear. The result of Eutyches' teaching was a confused mixture, not fully God or man.

The Council of Chalcedon

To settle this critical matter of how to view the two natures of Jesus, a major council of more than 400 church leaders was called at Chalcedon in 451. After much debate, these leaders affirmed a statement rooted in Scripture that has singularly remained the most important declaration about Jesus Christ in the history of the church.

The statement proclaimed Jesus to be both God and man in one person. It declared that both natures are joined in a miraculous way so neither nature is damaged, diminished, or impaired. His two natures are joined "unconfusedly, unchangeably, indivisibly, and inseparably" (Leith, 36). Salvation is thus secured for those who profess faith in Jesus because His sacrifice was as both saving God and identifying man.

From Chalcedon, then, the church taught that Jesus is undiminished deity plus perfect humanity united in one person, without any confusion of the two natures. In the absolute sense of the term, He is the God-man!

We live in a world where religious cults are threatening orthodox truth at every turn. If church history teaches us anything, it is this—precision of language in doctrinal matters is imperative. Any choice of words when describing Jesus that diminishes His deity or His humanity is incorrect and heretical.

The miracle of the Incarnation stretches our finite minds to the limit. The great legacy of the Council of Chalcedon reflects a consensus on the language that preserves both the complete deity and humanity of Jesus in His person. A complete salvation demands it; faith in the God-man, Jesus Christ, procures it.

AUGUSTINE—THEOLOGIAN OF GRACE

A quest for truth—no phrase better describes the work of the great theologian Augustine (354–430). After years of struggle with lust and doubt, he wrote of God: "You made us for Yourself, and our heart is restless until it finds rest in You" (*Confessions*, Book 1:1). His quest for truth found its satisfaction in the person of Christ, whose saving grace became the vital center of his theology. Augustine powerfully captured that personal search for truth in *The Confessions*, one of the truly profound spiritual autobiographies of history.

Born in northern Africa of a pagan father (Patricius) and a devout, godly mother (Monica), Augustine excelled as a student, especially in the ancient art of rhetoric. This introduced him to the genius of the Roman rhetorician, Cicero. Although Cicero was not a Christian, his writings started Augustine on his pursuit of truth and wisdom.

One of Augustine's greatest intellectual hurdles was the problem of evil—how could a good God permit a world filled with evil, pain, and suffering? He thought he had found the answer in Manichaeism. But when he examined Faustus, an important leader of the Manichees, his disillusionment with Faustus's arguments caused him to abandon the system. He tried other philosophies, but none satisfied his yearning for truth and wisdom.

Another intense battle of Augustine's early adulthood was with immorality and pride. For many years he kept a mistress, who bore him an illegitimate son. Because none of the philosophical systems he tried made demands on his personal morality, he believed his immoral lifestyle was justified. Too, his passion for personal fame in the academic world consumed him.

Seeking fame and fortune, Augustine traveled to Rome and Milan hoping to teach his beloved rhetoric. There he met Ambrose, the bishop of Milan. Ambrose's brilliance impressed Augustine, for Ambrose showed Augustine that his objections to Christianity were shallow and mistaken.

Augustine's conversion in 386 came, however, not through intellectual argumentation alone, but through an emotional encounter with the Almighty. In a garden outside Milan, he sat one day pondering the philosophical questions with which he had been toiling. As he tells it in his *Confessions*, he heard a child's voice say, "Take and read." He took up Paul's letter to the Romans (especially 13:13-14) and there found his questions answered. "All the shadows of doubt were swept away," he wrote (*Confessions*, Book 8:12). In God's Word, he found truth in the person of Jesus Christ. He also found the power to shatter his bondage to lust and self-seeking glory, and he found the peace and purpose for life that none of the intellectual fads of his day could provide. He experienced the power of God's grace that would define the rest of his life.

Augustine changed radically, breaking all ties with his immoral past. After Ambrose baptized him in 387, he returned to northern Africa where he embarked on a lifetime of study and devotion to Christ's church. He became a priest in 391 and in 395 the bishop of Hippo, a city west of Carthage. His enormous power and influence were felt for many years from that bishopric, especially through his voluminous writing.

Augustine's contributions to the church were extensive; in so many ways he was a transitional figure in church history. First, he defended the free-grace Gospel of Christ against many opponents, of which none was more threatening than Pelagius.

Pelagius, a British monk, taught a system that denied original sin and the need for God's grace in salvation, thereby championing a radical man-centered theology. Man, in effect, had the ability to save himself. Augustine leveled the definitive response at Pelagius. He affirmed the guilt and corruption of all humans because of Adam's sin and the absolute need for God's saving grace. Following Paul, Augustine formulated the doctrines of election and predestination that would powerfully influence Luther and Calvin centuries later. Augustine's theological system was God-centered, with salvation totally and causatively effected by God.

Second, Augustine's *Treatise on the Holy Trinity* is a magnificent theological masterpiece. In it he saw the God of the Bible as an eternal, transcendent, infinite, and perfect triune God. In defining God as a Trinity in one essence, his work constituted the capstone of centuries of theological thought on the nature of God. There was little debate on the nature of the Trinity after Augustine.

In his work on the Trinity, Augustine also solved his personal struggle with the problem of evil. For him, the Bible taught that God created the universe out of nothing (ex nihilo) and created humans and angels with a free will. Free will explained how evil entered into a good universe—Satan, some angels, and humans chose to rebel against God. Grace was the only explanation of why God chose to redeem humanity through His Son.

Third, his City of God, rooted in a belief in God's sovereignty and providence, postulated the first genuine Christian philosophy of history. Written as a response to the destruction of Rome in 410 by the Visigoths, this work saw history as a story of two cities—the city of God and the city of man.

Each city is motivated by contrary loves—the city of God by love for God and the city of man by love of self. Both will continue until the end, when God will bring eternal condemnation on the rebellious city and eternal salvation to the obedient one. Therefore, Augustine argued, Rome fell, as will all cities of man, because it was sinful, idolatrous, and rebellious. Only God's city will triumph.

Other aspects of Augustine's theology deserve comment. Because of his ascetic lifestyle, he found repugnant any reference to a literal millennial kingdom on earth. He rebelled against the idea of God bringing in a kingdom of material goodness and physical abundance. So he allegorized passages like Revelation 20 and taught that these verses referred to the present age, not a literal thousand-year reign of Christ.

In an age when intellectual fads and promiscuous lifestyles continue to enslave, the life of Augustine remains a compelling one. He demonstrated that only God's grace can break the chains of sin, for Jesus alone provides the answers to life's vexing questions. Once Augustine found life's key, he stood as a model of erudition and brilliance explained only by the power of God's grace.

The Theologians achieved doctrinal consensus on what the Scriptures taught about the Trinity and Jesus Christ. The matter of the roles of God and man in the dynamic of salvation was not as easy. Increasingly, the official position of the Roman Catholic Church rendered man's role as equally important, so that salvation was taught to be a cooperative effort between man and God.

FOR FURTHER DISCUSSION

1. Summarize Arius's beliefs about Jesus.
2. What were the three theological positions represented at the Council of Nicea?
3. What three words best summarize Athanasius's position on the members of the Trinity?
4. Summarize the work of the Three Cappadocians on the nature of the Trinity.
5. Where was the error of each of the following—Apollinarius, Nestorius, Eutyches?
6. What was the importance of the Council of Chalcedon in 451?
7. Summarize the differences between Augustine and Pelagius.

THE MEDIEVAL CHURCH

Jesus Christ . . . whose body and blood are truly contained
in the sacrament of the altar under the figures of bread
and wine, the bread having been transubstantiated into
His body and the wine into His blood by divine power.

FOURTH LATERAN COUNCIL, 1215

In church history the medieval church comprised the period from about 600 to 1517. The collapse of the western Roman Empire in the fifth century left an enormous vacuum in Western Europe. The political, economic, social, moral, and intellectual structures of an immense civilization no longer existed. Undeniably, the institutionalized Roman Catholic Church filled this vacuum. The papacy gained legitimacy, monasticism became entrenched, Islam exploded across the Mediterranean, and the Crusades resulted. As the church grew in influence and power though, it became corrupt and ineffective. This is the story of the medieval church.

GREGORY I AND THE PAPACY

Protestant church historians generally maintain that institutionalized Roman Catholicism began with Gregory's appointment as bishop of Rome in 590. Though he refused the title of pope, administratively he organized the papal system of government that characterized the entire medieval period. Thus all the major bishoprics of the West looked to him for guidance and leadership. He likewise standardized the liturgy and theology of the burgeoning Roman church. Doctrines such as the veneration of Mary, purgatory, an early form of transubstantiation, and praying to departed saints found their infant pronouncements in his writings.

Gregory also promoted missionary activity among the Germanic tribes. The various Germanic groups that had destroyed the western empire needed to hear the Gospel. Gregory's zeal for missions led him to send dozens of monks to northern Europe, especially England. Many in England came to Christ, and Canterbury became the English center of Catholicism. Gregory laid the foundation for the great edifice known as Roman Catholicism.

Two other factors contributed to the growing power and prestige of the Roman bishop. First, an early king of the Franks, Pepin the Short (714–768), granted the pope extensive land in central Italy—the Donation of Pepin—making the Catholic Church a temporal and political power in Europe. Second, the Donation of Constantine allegedly gave power and authority to the Roman bishop when Constantine relocated his capital to the East. The document was later discovered to be a forgery. Both, however, solidified the position of the pope.

MISSIONARY ACTIVITY TO THE GERMANIC TRIBES

A number of independent Germanic kingdoms, each ruled by a pagan king, replaced the mighty Roman Empire. In an attempt to reach these kingdoms for Christ, missionary activity exploded across Europe. The English missionary named Boniface (circa 672–754) was the greatest of these missionaries.

Born in the Anglo-Saxon kingdom of Wessex in the early 670s, his original name was Winfrid. He was trained in a Saxon monastic school in Exeter and exhibited a mastery of the Scriptures and the ministry skills of teaching and administration. By the age of thirty, he was ordained. At this point he developed a fervor for missions. His ambition was to join another missionary, Willibrord, in Frisia (the Netherlands).

Winfrid sought the support of both the bishop of Rome (by now largely accepted as the pope of the church) and the ruler of the Franks. He received the endorsement of both, gaining the Roman name of Boniface in the process. From Frisia he launched his missionary thrust into Germany, which would consume his energy for the remainder of his life.

Boniface ministered in the areas of Hesse and Thuringia and led thousands of pagan Germans to the Lord. Furthermore, where there had been nothing but idolatrous heathenism, he planted scores of churches. Symbolic of the triumph of Christianity over German paganism is the story of the felling of the Oak of Thor at Geismar in Hesse. Thor, the Nordic god of thunder, was revered by the Germans, and this oak tree was dedicated to his power and glory. With resolute zeal, Boniface chopped down the tree and used the wood for the foundation of a church dedicated to St. Peter.

He also brought remarkable organization to the burgeoning German church. In 732 the bishop of Rome appointed him archbishop over Germany. By pressing for an educated, disciplined, and pure clergy, Boniface systematically purged the German church of lazy, incompetent clerics and the lingering rites and rituals of German paganism. Using missionary volunteers from England, many of whom were women, he advanced organization and structure in the German church and filled it with zeal for obedience, service, and outreach.

Besides his administrative and missionary work, Boniface established monasteries throughout Germany, the most famous being at Fulda. Boniface was a Benedictine monk, who followed the Great Rule of Benedict of Nursia (the founder of monasticism in the West).The Benedictines emphasized poverty, chastity, and obedience to Christ. This rule became the norm for monastic communities throughout Europe. Monasteries became places of worship, devotion, prayer, and study— oases in the midst of pagan terror and decadence. Monks copied the Scriptures and early Christian classics. In fact, monasteries were the only educational centers during much of the medieval period. Over the hundreds of years of medieval civilization, however, these places of self-denial gradually became places of immorality, self-indulgence, and materialistic pursuit. The ones Boniface founded were largely places of education, hospitality, and missionary outreach. It is clear that God used them.

Boniface also nurtured the growing relationship between Franks and the church centered in Rome. The bishop of Rome needed protection, and the king of the Franks was willing to give it. Boniface secured special recognition from the pope for the Frankish king, Pepin, thereby nourishing what would flower into a powerful church-state alliance much later in the medieval period.

MISSIONARY ACTIVITY IN IRELAND

Similar pioneer work was done by Patrick (circa 389–461) among the Irish people. As Celts, the Irish people had never been a part of the

Roman Empire. Although they had contacts with Britain, the Irish Celts were culturally, economically, and politically different. As Rome declined, it abandoned Britain as too difficult to defend; so the church filled the vacuum. The spiritual outreach to Ireland was primarily the work of Patrick.

He was born in Britain in 389, apparently to an affluent Christian family. Tragically, at the age of sixteen, he was kidnapped and sold into slavery in northern Ireland, where he worked as a shepherd and farmer. Yet in God's sovereignty, his conversion to Christ dates from this period. He wrote in *The Confession* that God opened his eyes and "showed him his sins."

After six years in slavery, he escaped, eventually ending up back in Britain. There, he apparently furthered his education and received a vision from the Lord calling him back to the Irish people who had enslaved him. As an itinerant minister, he understood the evangelistic dynamic of the Christian faith. He discerned that it alone offered what the Druid priests could not—peace to a land troubled by tribal warfare. He, therefore, developed a strategy for winning the tribal leaders of Ireland to Christ. All evidence indicates that many local lords and kings became Christians. As they converted, they guaranteed protection for the successful spread of the faith throughout Ireland. Some estimates suggest more than 100,000 converts as a result of Patrick's ministry.

Additionally, the Irish church became a missionary-sending church. From the strategic island of Iona, where a notable monastery existed, Columba (521–597) launched out to convert the Scots and Picts of Scotland and the Angles and Saxons of northern England. Columba became one of the greatest missionaries in church history. But without Patrick, there would have been no Columba, for Patrick led Columba's grandfather to Christ and baptized him.

God thus used Patrick to transform Ireland from a land saturated with the secretive magic and the occultist practices of the Druids to one devoted to Christ and His kingdom.

ISLAM

During the sixth and seventh centuries, the rise of a new monotheistic faith—Islam—drew great numbers of members away from the Roman Catholic Church. The religion centers on Mohammed (circa 570–632), the prophet of Allah, who claimed he had received a series of revelations from the angel Gabriel. Those revelations were later inscripturated in the Qur'an (Koran). The hub of the Qur'an, called the Witness, is that there is one God, Allah, and Mohammed is his prophet. To say this in faith is to become a Muslim, one who submits to God.

In addition to reciting the Witness, Muslims observe four other pillars of faith. Devout Muslims pray five times daily, pay alms to the poor, fast during the daylight hours of the month of Ramadan, and make a pilgrimage to Mecca. The theology of Islam thus concentrates on winning the favor of Allah through the practice of the faith.

Islam spread quickly. As Mohammed preached faith in Allah, he met tremendous resistance and in 622 fled from Mecca to Medina—the most important event in Islamic history. By 630 he had reconquered Mecca and established control over much of the Arabian peninsula. By 732 his successors had overcome Palestine, northern Africa, and Spain and were only stopped at the Battle of Tours in France. The military vacuum left by the collapse of western Rome and the jihad, or holy war, proclaimed by the Qur'an, help to explain the swift conquest of Islam. Huge territories once dominated by Christianity were lost, many of which have never been recovered.

"NE'ER THE TWAIN SHALL MEET"

After the fall of Rome, the Eastern and Western wings of the Roman Catholic Church faced differing circumstances. With no emperor to interfere, the Western popes gained power as they dealt with the chaos left by the barbarian invaders. By contrast, the Eastern Empire's ruler interfered in the affairs of the Eastern church, which also had to spend resources and energy fighting Islam.

The two branches of the church also took different positions on a number of issues. In the second century they had disagreed over when to celebrate Easter. They also differed on the issue of celibacy for clergy below the rank of bishop and on the use of statues and pictures of saints in churches. The most serious disagreement came in 867 when the Eastern patriarch accused the Western church of heresy for saying that the Holy Spirit proceeded from the Father and the Son rather than just from the Father.

Relations between the two churches became increasingly hostile until a minor issue brought the factions into a confrontation in 1054. All the bitter feelings and differences from the past erupted in the discussion. The meeting ended with the Roman delegates excommunicating the patriarch and his followers. Not to be outdone, the patriarch anathematized the pope and the Western church. From that time on the Roman

Catholic Church and the Greek Orthodox Church have gone in different directions.

THE CRUSADES

Muslims were predominantly Arabs until the eleventh century when the Seljuk Turks assumed control over much of Islamic territory. Much more fanatical and brutal, the Turks harassed Christian pilgrims and threatened the security of the Eastern church. Hence, in 1095 Pope Urban II issued a call to deliver the holy places of Palestine from Muslim hands. The response of Christian Europe was overwhelming. From 1095 to 1291, waves of Christian warriors set out to accomplish Urban's goal. Few of the Crusades were successful.

There were seven major crusades, with dozens of smaller ones. The first crusade (1095–1099) was the only successful one. The crusaders established the Latin Kingdom in Jerusalem, which lasted several decades. They built castles to defend their holdings and organized several orders of knights to protect the holy places. But their effort was in vain. Gradually, the Muslims regained control of Palestine and drove out the Christians.

The Crusades radically transformed Christian Europe. Culturally, as crusaders returned from the East, they brought new foods and clothing with them. Educationally, books from the ancient world that had been preserved by the Muslim Arabs became available to Europeans. Economically, trade revived, the church gained new wealth from the wills of soldiers lost in battle, and a new class—the middle class—began to take hold in the West. Politically, as kings taxed their subjects to gain revenue, their power increased. In many ways, the Crusades were a defining moment in the medieval church. People's loyalties were no longer directed solely toward the church. Over time the church was simply not as important in their lives as it once was.

ROMAN CATHOLIC SCHOLASTIC THEOLOGY

Key questions throughout church history have been these: Reason and faith—are they enemies or allies? Is the Christian faith reasonable, or is it simply a blind leap that is ultimately irrational? A major advance in answering these questions came with the emergence of a group of medieval theologians called the Scholastics. Prominent among them was Anselm of Canterbury (1033–1109) and Thomas Aquinas (circa 1225–1274).

Anselm devoted most of his adult life to suggesting reasonable arguments for theological propositions he had already embraced as truth by faith. His goal was not to attain faith through reason; rather, he wanted to use reason as a tool to better understand what he already believed. For Anselm, faith preceded and guided reason. He wrote in *Proslogion,* "I believe in order to understand." Through reason he sought to strengthen and give understanding to his faith. His was a "faith seeking understanding."

In his writings, Anselm gave reasonable proofs for God's existence and compelling reasons for God as the self-existent, incorporeal, almighty, compassionate, just, and merciful one. In his book *Why the Godman?* Anselm also demonstrated the crucial interrelationship between the incarnation of God's Son and His atonement for sin. His argument that Christ's atonement infinitely satisfied God powerfully influenced the thinking of Luther and Calvin centuries later.

The apex of Scholastic theology, however, was reached with Thomas Aquinas. His life of scholarship forever shaped the direction of institutionalized Catholicism. So profound was his influence that he earned the nickname "The Angelic Doctor." His magnum opus was *Summa Theologica.* In the *Summa* he maintained that philosophical reasoning and faith were perfect complements: Reason leads one to the "vestibule of faith."

Aquinas gave critical support to the distinctive doctrines of the Christian faith, including the attributes of God, the Resurrection, and *ex nihilo* creation. However, his defense of the veneration of Mary, purgatory, the role of human merit in salvation, and the seven holy sacraments through which God conveys grace are without biblical support. In addition, his idea that the Communion elements at the prayer of consecration become sacrificially the actual body and blood of Christ was rejected by Luther and the other sixteenth-century reformers as unbiblical.

THE CHURCH ON THE EVE OF THE REFORMATION

The Roman Catholic Church of the fourteenth and fifteenth centuries experienced a crisis of authority. Upheaval within and remarkable pressures from without undermined its credibility and legitimacy. The result was that the church was positioned for the Reformation of the sixteenth century.

Due to the politics of late medieval Europe, Clement V relocated the seat of the papacy to Avignon, France, in 1309. Under the dominance of France, the Avignon papacy was nicknamed the "Babylonian Captivity of the Church." Attempts to end this intolerable situation produced two duly-elected popes, one in Avignon and one in Rome, in what was called the Great Schism (1378–1417). Finally, the Council of Constance, with the insistence of the Holy Roman Emperor, ended the schism. The solution, however, raised serious questions about the authority of the papacy, further dividing the church leaders.

In addition to these political questions, the church was racked by corruption and fraud. Clergy bought and sold church offices (simony). Immorality among church leaders who professed celibacy further heightened the crisis of confidence. The church likewise spent a fortune acquiring thousands of relics for its cathedrals and paying for them with the selling of forgiveness (indulgences). The church thus became an object of ridicule and satire in pamphlets and books that were readily available with the invention of the printing press.

In the fourteenth and fifteenth centuries, mysticism also challenged the church from within. Most significant was the Brethren of Common Life and the Brethren's most famous spokesman, Thomas à Kempis. The Brethren stood in opposition to the Catholic monastic orders and breathed new spiritual life into the church. They stressed personal devotion to Jesus through study and meditation, confession of sin, and imitating Christ. They likewise emphasized obedience, holiness, and simplicity. In many ways, the Brethren prefigured the reformers of the sixteenth century.

Availability of the written Word of God also undermined the church. John Wycliffe (circa 1329–1384) believed that the Bible was the final authority for the believer and that each believer should have an opportunity to read it. But the only available version was the Latin Bible known as the Vulgate. So Wycliffe and his associates translated that Latin Bible into English. Wycliffe also wrote tracts arguing that Christ, not the pope, was the head of the church, that priests were unnecessary, and that the Catholic belief that the bread and wine became the literal body and blood of Christ was wrong.

The sixteenth-century world was one of astounding change. Medieval civilization dominated by institutionalized Catholicism was disappearing. Modern nation-states challenged the church for supremacy, and the voyages of discovery made the world appear smaller. In addition, the Renaissance of northern Italy had caused many to turn from Catholicism toward the glories of ancient Greece and Rome. Into this changing world stepped Desiderius Erasmus (1466–1536).

Erasmus found it quite easy to ridicule the Catholic church. In his most famous example, *Praise of Folly* (1509), he took jabs at the church's pervasive immorality, corruption, and decadence. He ridiculed its superstitions such as fanatical devotion to relics, stories of bleeding hosts, and the cult of saints. In another tract, he depicted Saint Peter castigating Pope Julius II for his life of luxury, military conquest, and opulence, and denying him entrance into heaven.

In 1516 Erasmus published his most influential work—his Greek edition of the New Testament. He examined and compared some of the available New Testament manuscripts and citations from the Church Fathers. The result was an accurate New Testament Greek text that became the New Testament of the Reformation. Although overstated, the old epigram, "Erasmus laid the egg that Luther hatched," captures the influence of Erasmus.

By the sixteenth century, reform of the church seemed imminent. All that was needed was the right individual. Martin Luther was that man. He provided the spark for the most significant reform in the history of the church.

FOR FURTHER DISCUSSION

1. Explain why Protestants consider Gregory I to be the first pope of the Roman Catholic Church.
2. What is monasticism, and what were some positive aspects of this movement?
3. How did God use Boniface and Patrick in the early medieval church?
4. Summarize the theology of Islam and explain why it spread so quickly.
5. Summarize the reasons why the church separated into East and West in 1054.
6. What were the Crusades and their results?
7. What were the contributions of Anselm and Aquinas?

THE REFORMATION CHURCH

Unless I am convicted of error . . . by the Scriptures to which
I have appealed, and my conscience is taken captive by
God's Word, I cannot and will not recant of anything,
for to act against our conscience is neither safe for us,
nor open to us. Here I stand. I can do no other.
May God help me! Amen.

MARTIN LUTHER, DIET OF WORMS, 1521

As the preceding chapter makes clear, by the sixteenth century, the spirit of reform permeated Europe. The only question was whether Christendom could survive intact. Events in sixteenth-century Germany answered the question.

MARTIN LUTHER

Luther was born November 10, 1483, in Eisleben, Germany, into an affluent copper miner's family. Steered firmly by his father, Luther decided to seek a degree in law. But one July day in 1505, a violent thunderstorm knocked him to the ground, and he screamed, "Help me, St. Anne! I will become a monk" (Bainton, 1950, 78). That vow changed his life.

To his father's consternation, Luther joined the Augustinian cloister in Erfurt. There he opened and studied the Bible for the first time.

His fervent yearning to serve, please, and love God stemmed from a haunting fear of God's judgment. To win God's favor, he committed himself to a rigorous schedule of study, meditation, and fasting. But his life of rigid asceticism brought no peace. God was his judge, not his Savior.

In 1511 his Augustinian order sent him to the University of Wittenberg where he completed his Th.D. in October 1512. He then secured a permanent appointment there as a professor of Bible. But his struggle over God's holiness and justice deepened. Sometime between 1517 and 1519 Luther found the peace he sought. Through reading the New Testament, especially Romans, he came to understand that justification was not by works but through faith. Neither Luther nor the world would ever be the same.

Across the river from Wittenberg, a Dominican monk named Johann Tetzel was selling indulgences. These were small pieces of parchment that guaranteed forgiveness of sins for a price. Brazenly he trumpeted, "As soon as the coin in the coffer rings, the soul from purgatory springs." Such arrogance enraged Luther. He preached fervently against indulgences, and on October 31, 1517, he nailed Ninety-Five Theses for debate on the Castle Church door at Wittenberg. In them he argued that indulgences could not remove guilt, did not apply to purgatory, and provided a false sense of security. He later wrote, "The pope has no jurisdiction over purgatory, and if he does, he should empty the place free of charge" (Bainton, 1950, 81). The Reformation had begun.

From 1517 to 1521 Luther's stand against the church hardened. In 1520 when Pope Leo excommunicated him, Luther publicly burned the order. Furthermore, his writings from this period reflected a distinctly non-Catholic theology. He argued that Scripture allowed for only two ordinances—baptism and the Lord's Supper. He also rejected the Catholic dogma of transubstantiation. Justification came by faith alone; works played no role in salvation.

The most serious challenge to Luther came when the new Holy Roman emperor, Charles V, ordered him to answer charges at the imperial Diet of Worms. When asked to recant his writings, Luther responded, "Unless I am convicted of error . . . by the Scriptures to which I have appealed, and my conscience is taken captive by God's Word, I cannot and will not recant of anything, for to act against our conscience is neither safe for us, nor open to us. Here I stand. I can do no other. May God help me! Amen!"

With his life now in jeopardy, friends "kidnapped" him and took him secretly to Wartburg Castle. While there, he translated the New Testament from the Greek into German. Meanwhile, the revolt against the Roman Catholic Church spread. Towns all over Germany removed religious statues, abolished the mass, and forced priests from churches. As princes of the Holy Roman Empire chose to support the Lutheran cause the Reformation became a political issue as well.

After a year at Wartburg, Luther went back to Wittenberg where he taught and preached for the rest of his life. In 1525 he married Catherine von Bora, a former nun, who bore him six children. He continued to write prolifically, including theology books, Bible commentaries, and music. As a pastor, he sought a method by which God's Word could endure in the hearts of his people. The singing of hymns met that need. He reshaped ancient tunes and melodies into dozens of hymns, such as "A Mighty Fortress Is Our God" and "Away in a Manger."

Luther's close friend and disciple, Philip Melanchthon (1497–1560), emerged as the theologian of Lutheranism. He authored the *Augsburg Confession* (1530) and its *Apology*, both forceful statements of early Protestant theology. But as a courteous and timid peacemaker, Melanchthon attempted to steer a middle course in early theological debates of the Reformation. Rarely did he satisfy anyone. In that sense, he personifies the tension caused by theological debate.

ZWINGLI

Ulrich Zwingli was born in Wildhaus, Switzerland, in 1484. Educated in the best universities and ordained a priest, Zwingli seemed destined to serve his life in the priesthood. But through theological inquiry and personal struggle, he came to saving faith in 1516. By 1523 he was leading the Reformation in Zurich. In 1526 his teaching and preaching convinced the city council to permit clergy to marry, abolish the mass, ban Catholic images and statues, dissolve the monasteries, and sever all ties with Rome. Additionally, the Zurich reformers published their vernacular New Testament in 1524 and the entire Bible in 1530, four years before Luther's translation became available.

Breaking his vow of celibacy, Zwingli secretly married Anna Reinhart in 1522. He made their wedding public in 1524. Like Luther, he demonstrated that spiritual leadership did not demand celibacy. His break with Rome was radical.

Zwingli was at the center of a major theological debate concerning the Lord's Table. Between 1525 and 1528 a bitter "pamphlet war" ensued between the Zwinglians and the Lutherans. Both sides rejected the

Roman Catholic doctrine of transubstantiation—that the priest's prayer transformed the elements into the literal, sacrificial body and blood of Christ. Their disagreement centered on Jesus' words, "This is My body." The Lutherans maintained that Jesus was present "in, with, and under" (from the *Augsburg Confession*) the elements and that participation in the sacrament strengthened the believer spiritually (consubstantiation). The Zwinglians regarded this as an unnecessary compromise with Catholicism. Instead, they concluded that because Christ's physical body was no longer present on earth, His words must be understood symbolically. The elements represented Jesus' body, and Communion was merely a memorial. The debate remains unsettled today.

Zwingli believed the state and church should reinforce one another in the work of God; there should be no separation. Therefore, the Reformation became increasingly political and split Switzerland into Catholic and Protestant cantons (or states). Warfare resulted. At the battle of Cappel (1531), a coalition of five Catholic cantons defeated Zurich. Zwingli, the chaplain for the Zurich forces, was killed during the battle. When his enemies discovered his body, they quartered and burned it. His ardor for reform had cost him his life.

CALVIN

With Zwingli dead, the Swiss reformers lacked a leader. John Calvin (1509–1564) filled that gap. As the reformer of Geneva, he inspired John Knox, the Dutch Reformation, the English Reformation, and the Puritans and Pilgrims of North America.

Calvin was born in France on July 10, 1509, and studied theology at the University of Paris and law at the University of Orleans. Sometime during the 1520s he trusted Christ and joined the young Protestant cause. An explosion of anti-Protestant fury forced Calvin to flee Paris. For three years he was on the run in France, Switzerland, and Italy.

During this time he also began writing. By March 1536 he had published *Institutes of the Christian Religion*. At first a slim volume, the *Institutes* went through five revisions. The 1559 edition is the definitive one containing four books of eighty chapters. With its theme of "God, the Creator and Sovereign Ruler of the World," it was the systematic theology of the Reformation.

Calvin eventually ended up in Geneva. The city council appointed him to lead the Reformation, but he never held political office and did not become a citizen until 1559. His goal was to make Geneva a "holy commonwealth" where the laws of God would be the laws of man. He preached every day and twice on Sunday. He established an academy for training the youth of the city and arranged for the care of the poor and the aged. Calvin's Geneva was a commonwealth of doctrine and practice and a model of Reformation living.

Because Geneva was so strategically located, Protestant refugees from all over Catholic Europe flooded into the city. They sat under Calvin's teaching, and when they returned home, they took his theology with them. This pattern explains the remarkable spread of Calvinism throughout the Western world.

In addition to his amazing preaching and teaching schedule, Calvin also wrote prolifically. He wrote lectures, theological treatises, and commentaries on thirty-three books of the Old Testament and the entire New Testament except Revelation. As Philip Schaff has written, "Calvin was the founder of the modern historical-grammatical exegesis" of God's Word (Schaff, 8:118-119). The reformer likewise carried on a massive correspondence with people all over Europe.

Calvin is often pictured as a disciplined, authoritarian fanatic. This idea is quite inaccurate. He loved life. He loved to play games and frequently visited the homes of his followers. He also spent many hours giving premarital counseling in his church. But it was his participation in the execution of Michael Servetus that contributed most to the image of Calvin as an extremist.

Servetus, a Spaniard, was already under the ban of the Catholic church for his heretical teaching—principally his denial of the Trinity. The Genevan city fathers imprisoned Servetus. In an attempt to convert him, Calvin made several unsuccessful visits to his cell. So with the full support of other Swiss Protestant cities, Geneva executed Servetus in 1553.

Because Calvin believed so strongly in the sovereignty of God, he held that God was directly involved in all aspects of the drama of salvation, including predestination and election. Calvinism, which was later systematized by his followers, is a God-centered system of theology. Today Calvinism is often summarized with the acrostic TULIP:

T	-	Total Depravity
U	-	Unconditional Election
L	-	Limited Atonement
I	-	Irresistible Grace
P	-	Perseverance of the Saints.

Calvinism today is found in historic Presbyterianism, Reformed faiths, and some Baptist groups.

THE ANABAPTISTS

As a term, *anabaptist* means "to again baptize." The Anabaptist movement stressed believer's baptism, as opposed to infant baptism. But the term also refers to widely diverse groups of Reformers, many of which embraced quite radical social, political, economic, and religious views. The most respectable groups included the Swiss Brethren, the Mennonites, the Hutterites, and the Amish.

When it comes to the tenets of Protestant theology, most Anabaptist groups adhered to sound teaching on the Scriptures, the Trinity, justification by faith, and the atonement of Jesus Christ. Many Anabaptists, however, maintained several distinctives that made them objects of persecution by both Catholics and some Protestants. First, nearly all championed believer's baptism—a rejection of infant baptism, which Catholicism and most other Protestant groups affirmed. Second, most argued for a gathered church concept as opposed to a state church. Third, as a corollary, many defended the separation of church and state. Fourth, some taught that Christians should live communally and share all material possessions. Fifth, many supported the position of nonresistance and sometimes pacifism. Finally, many Anabaptists preached a strict form of church discipline. Each of these marked Anabaptism as a movement quite distinct from all other Reformation groups.

Zwingli's zeal produced intolerance, especially toward the Anabaptists. Two of his disciples, Conrad Grebel and Felix Manz, were impatient for radical reform. They became critical of Zwingli's relationship with the city council and broke with Zwingli over the nature of baptism. Essentially, Grebel and Manz founded the Anabaptist movement. Because their beliefs were clearly antagonistic to Zwingli and the city council, the Anabaptists were fined, imprisoned, and martyred by the Swiss authorities.

THE ENGLISH REFORMATION

As a nation, England was ripe for reformation. The work of Wycliffe and his followers, the Lollards, had prepared the way. The writings of Luther circulated through the land. In addition, William Tyndale (1494–1536) and Miles Coverdale (1488–1568) had each produced highly accurate translations of the Bible that were widely available. But the catalyst for the break with Rome came with the marital problems of the English king, Henry VIII.

Henry's marriage to Catherine of Aragon had produced no sons; how ever, Henry's affair with Anne Boleyn resulted in her pregnancy. When Henry sought an annulment of his marriage, the pope refused. In 1534 Henry, therefore, removed England from the pope's jurisdiction and made himself head of the English church (now called the Anglican church). Henry also confiscated Catholic land.

As Protestant and Catholic forces in England struggled for control, confusion and crisis reigned for the next decade. But when Elizabeth I, Henry's daughter, came to the throne, she chose a middle road built upon national unity and not theological considerations. The core of her solution was that the Anglican church would be Protestant in its theology and Catholic in its ritual. She therefore neutralized Catholicism in England but did not satisfy her most vocal critics, the Puritans.

Puritanism was a complex movement that primarily yearned for the purification of the Anglican church. Puritans wanted to complete the Reformation in England. They claimed that Elizabeth had not gone far enough in her reforms. Congregational in church government and Calvinist in theology, the Puritans would later be expelled from the Anglican church. This, in turn, led to the emigration of many to North America.

JOHN KNOX AND SCOTLAND

Frequently shifting its allegiance between France and England, Scotland was caught in the vice of geopolitical conflict. The Reformation fed this instability. At the center of this conflict was John Knox (1514–1572).

Fearing the spreading Reformation, the Catholics in control of Scotland appealed to France for help. Therefore, on July 31, 1547, the French navy arrived at St. Andrews, seized the stronghold, and took all the occupants back to France. Among those seized was Knox. Efforts to propagandize him with Catholic doctrine failed. His enslavement became the watershed event of his life. He became a revolutionary for the cause of Christ.

Released from slavery after nineteen months, Knox fled to England where he joined the Reformation forces committed to Thomas Cranmer. For more than two years, he became an itinerant evangelist, proclaiming the Reformation gospel in Berwick and Newcastle. But the "Boy-King," Edward VI (a devout Protestant and enamored with Knox), died in 1553, making Mary Tudor (a steadfast Catholic) queen.

She became known as "Bloody Mary," and her reign centered on the systematic and ruthless persecution of Protestants. Hence, Knox fled to Germany.

During his exile in Europe (1554–1559), Knox pastored a church of exiles in Frankfurt, Germany, and developed a close relationship with John Calvin and other reformers. Knox's pastorate in Geneva was his most productive, for he helped translate the critical Geneva Bible, one of the first true study Bibles that included notes, maps, and prayers.

He also wrote his famous *The First Blast of the Trumpet Against the Monstrous Regiment of Women*, a biting polemic directed at Queen Mary and her Catholic following. In this pamphlet Knox developed his position on the rights of citizens in the face of an unjust ruler. Did they have the right to overthrow that ruler? Knox answered yes. He based his argument on Scripture, especially the case of Athaliah (2 Kings 11), who was overthrown and executed under orders from Jehoiada the priest. Knox also argued that when a ruler does not support the true church, referring to Queen Mary, that ruler's throne should be in jeopardy.

With the country on the verge of civil war, he returned to Scotland in May 1559 to lead the Protestant cause. As a result of complicated political moves on many fronts, the war did break out and soon drew in England and France. Knox was the heart and soul of the Protestant forces—as enlistment officer and even as a spy for the English behind French lines. The war ended in 1560, and the Treaty of Edinburgh recognized Presbyterianism. The new Parliament adopted the First Scottish Confession, written by Knox and others, as the theological confession of Scotland. It remained so until the famous Westminster Confession of 1647.

The spirit of reform impacted Catholicism as well. As the Catholic church responded to the advances of Protestantism, it built on reforms begun even before Luther appeared on the scene. That response is usually called the Catholic Counter-Reformation, the subject of the next chapter.

FOR FURTHER DISCUSSION

1. Why is October 31, 1517, so important to the Reformation?
2. Summarize Luther's disagreement with the Catholic church.
3. Zwingli's contribution to the Reformation centered on the Lord's Table. What was his view?

4. John Calvin's influence was immense. What was his role as leader in Geneva?
5. Summarize Calvin's teaching represented by the acrostic TULIP.
6. Who were the Anabaptists? What were some of the distinctive beliefs of this movement?
7. Detail the role that Henry VIII and his daughter Elizabeth played in the English Reformation.
8. Who was the undisputed leader of the Scottish Reformation?

THE CATHOLIC CHURCH
RESPONDS

If anyone says that the sinner is justified by faith alone . . .
let him be anathema.

COUNCIL OF TRENT, 1563

The Roman Catholic Church of the sixteenth century did not suddenly react to Protestantism. The spirit of reform was already present in Spain. However, the energy and zeal of Protestantism put Catholicism on the defensive and caused it to respond aggressively. That response was the Catholic Counter-Reformation.

SPAIN

In Spain the spirit of Catholic reform predated Martin Luther. The enthusiasm from evicting the Muslims and the persistence of medieval piety and mysticism fueled reform of the church there. When Queen Isabella began her rule of Castile in 1474, she brought a zeal to reform Spanish Catholicism and quickly gained papal approval for her fervor. Cardinal Francisco Jimenez (1436–1517), archbishop of Toledo, emerged as Isabella's key supporter in reorganizing Spanish Catholicism. In a campaign for holiness, Jimenez and Isabella set out to cleanse the monasteries and convents of Spain. They demanded renewal of monastic vows, enforced poverty among the clergy, emphasized the necessity of an educated clergy, and purged the monasteries of corruption and immorality.

Jimenez and Isabella also demanded high standards for scholarship, which both believed was the key to effective leadership. Therefore, they founded the University of Alcala, outside Madrid, which became an indispensable center of Spanish religious and literary life. The University of Alcala was likewise instrumental in publishing a new multilingual edition of the Bible, which included Scripture in Hebrew, Greek, and the Latin Vulgate—all in parallel columns. Jimenez said of the work that "this edition of the Bible . . . opens the sacred sources of our religion, from which flow a much purer theology than any derived from less direct sources" (Gonzalez, 2:112). Through this 1520 publication, Jimenez and Isabella affirmed the supremacy of Scripture over church tradition.

The Spanish Reformation was, however, hardly a model of tolerance. The pope gave Isabella and her husband, Ferdinand, authority to use the Inquisition, a church court, to enforce adherence to church doctrine and practices. The Jews were special victims of Spanish intolerance. In 1492 the Spanish crown decreed that all Jews must either accept Christian baptism or leave Spanish territories. Over 200,000 Jews fled Spain as a result, most losing their land, their possessions, and some even their lives. The Spanish crown passed similar laws aimed at Spanish Muslims, called Moors. Jimenez, now Grand Inquisitor, ruthlessly pursued the forced conversion of the Moors.

THE JESUITS

Several new monastic orders added to the energy emanating from Catholic Spain. None was more influential than the Society of Jesus (the Jesuits) founded by Spaniard Ignatius Loyola (1491–1556). Ignatius lived a life of luxury and pleasure until he was severely wounded in battle. That wound made him limp for the rest of his life. While recuperating from his wounds, he devoured religious literature, and in 1522 dedicated his life to God and the church. Such devotion led to the founding of the Jesuits in 1534. Patterned after the military, the Jesuit organization responded efficiently and rapidly to the challenges and opportunities of the Roman Catholic Church.

The mission of the Jesuits was threefold—education, fighting heresy, and missions. Through its teaching and preaching, the Jesuits regained control of parts of Germany and central Europe for the Catholic church. Francis Xavier (1506–1552) was the outstanding Jesuit missionary, ministering in Japan, the Far East, the East Indies, and parts of North America. Jesuit missionaries baptized thousands into the Roman Catholic faith.

Jesuit attacks against heresy meant attacks against Protestantism.

Jesuits utilized two weapons—the Index of Prohibited Books and the Inquisition. By publishing a list of books Catholics were not permitted to read, the Index controlled the minds of the faithful. The Inquisition, a church court originally established in 1490, rarely followed due process and often utilized torture. Its major objective was to obtain a confession and the retraction of heretical beliefs from the accused heretic. If found guilty, the accused faced imprisonment or execution. The Inquisitor's court rarely showed mercy. In Italy, Spain, Portugal, and Belgium the Inquisition successfully eradicated any Protestant threat.

PAUL III

The most important pope of the Counter-Reformation was Paul III, who served from 1534 to 1549. An enigmatic man, Paul seemed to trust astrology more than Catholic theology. Like other popes of the Renaissance period, he was immoral and strove to make Rome a glorious city of wealth and prestige. But he was also a reformer. He recognized the Jesuits as a legal church order in 1540, appointed dedicated men as cardinals of the church, and organized a committee of nine to investigate abuses in the church and to recommend reforms. But most importantly, he called the Council of Trent in 1545.

THE COUNCIL OF TRENT

The Council of Trent was the definitive Catholic response to Protestantism. From 1545 to 1563, for a total of 25 sessions, the council of bishops deliberated. The council conceded that Protestantism resulted from the "ambition, avarice, and cupidity" of Catholic bishops. It also ordered the systematic education and training of the clergy in established Catholic seminaries. In the seminaries, the church promoted the study of Thomas Aquinas, making him the dominant Catholic theologian. In a direct response to the Lutherans, the council likewise abolished indulgence sellers, listed and defined clergy obligations, regulated the use of relics, and ordered the restructuring of bishops within the church.

The doctrinal work of Trent is summarized in the Tridentine Profession of Faith, which championed Roman Catholic dogma and provided the major theological response to the Protestants. Trent rejected justification by faith alone and promoted the necessity of meritorious works as necessary in the dynamic of salvation. It also reaffirmed the seven grace-conveying sacraments instituted by Christ—baptism, confirmation, communion, penance, extreme unction, ordination, and marriage—as needed for sanctification. Trent also reaffirmed transubstantiation and the sacrificial nature of the mass, clearly rejecting all Protestant positions on the Lord's Table. Finally, it declared the Vulgate Bible alone as acceptable for church use and maintained that church tradition was equal in authority with Scripture. Clearly, the Tridentine statement made reconciliation with Protestantism impossible.

CATHOLIC SPIRITUALITY

Medieval mysticism and spirituality also contributed a new energy to institutionalized Catholicism. Throughout Catholic Europe, an emphasis on prayer, meditation, examination of conscience, reading of Scripture, and fellowship with God surfaced. Much of this fresh vigor predated Martin Luther and was quite critical of the church hierarchy. Thomas à Kempis's *The Imitation of Christ* and Ignatius's *Spiritual Exercises* exemplify the literature of Catholic spirituality that burst across Catholic Europe.

THE THIRTY YEARS' WAR

The Reformation sparked a whole series of religious wars across the European continent. All were bloody and dreadful. The last of these was the Thirty Years' War (1618–1648). The Peace of Augsburg of 1555 had put Lutheranism on a legal basis with Roman Catholicism in Germany. The prince of a region was to determine the religion in his territory, but any dissenters could emigrate to another territory. To preserve Catholic domination of southern Germany, the agreement mandated that Catholic rulers who became Lutherans had to surrender rule. The agreement also left out Calvinists, Anabaptists, and other Protestants. In many respects, Augsburg solved nothing.

Beginning in Bohemia, the Thirty Years' War ravaged Central Europe and Germany and involved all the major European powers. The Peace of Westphalia, which ended the war in 1648, resulted from long and complicated negotiations. France and Sweden gained large amounts of territory, and German princes gained greater power and influence at the expense of the emperor. The treaty also recognized Calvinism, along with the Lutherans and Catholics, as a legal religion and permitted each ruler to determine the religion of his state. The Reformation was over.

But the effects of the War were devastating for Christianity. Religious issues were increasingly treated with indifference by political leaders. Secular, self-serving matters were now the chief concerns of the growing worldly nation-states. The barbarity and brutality of the war left many questioning the Christian Gospel. How could a faith that produced such atrocities be true? Doctrine took a backseat to doubt and skepticism.

In the Catholic Counter-Reformation institutionalized Catholicism honestly came to terms with its own shortcomings and responded to the threat of Protestantism. Most of the offensive tactics of the Counter-Reformation eventually ended—the Inquisition in 1854 and the Index in 1966. But the Tridentine Profession of Faith dogmatized Catholic theological distinctives and rendered reconciliation with the Protestants impossible. Now both Catholics and Protestants faced a new threat—the modern world. The intellectual framework for modernism is the subject of the next two chapters.

FOR FURTHER DISCUSSION

1. Why can we say that the Catholic Counter-Reformation began before Luther?
2. Why were the Jesuits so important to the Catholic response to Protestantism? What weapons did they use?
3. Which pope called the Council of Trent?
4. Why did the Tridentine Profession of Faith make reconciliation with the Protestants nearly impossible?
5. What religious war ended the Reformation? How did this last religious war affect Christianity?

The Seven Sacraments
of the Roman Catholic Church

Reaffirmed at the Council of Trent (A.D. 1545–1563)

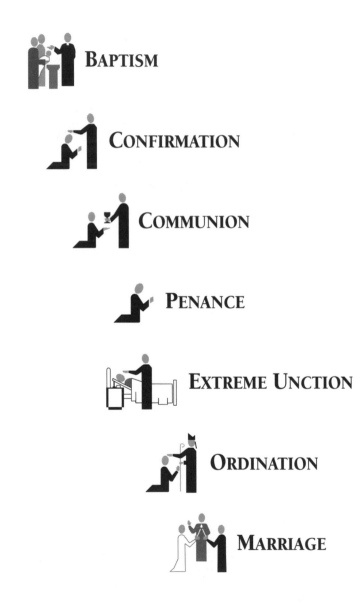

BAPTISM

CONFIRMATION

COMMUNION

PENANCE

EXTREME UNCTION

ORDINATION

MARRIAGE

THE CHURCH AND THE SCIENTIFIC REVOLUTION

Nature and Nature's Laws lay hid in Night;
God said, "Let Newton be," and All was Light.

ALEXANDER POPE

➣

The Scientific Revolution of the seventeenth century gave birth to modern culture. Modern science was both a product of the Reformation and the beginning of modern naturalism, which rejects the role of the supernatural in the physical world. How did this development occur?

THE REFORMATION AND MODERN SCIENCE

The Reformation challenged the authority of Roman Catholicism, which had dogmatized as theology a particular scientific view of the world. That view of the world is often called the Aristotelian-Ptolemaic model, built on the thinking of the Greek philosopher Aristotle (384–322 B.C.) and the second-century A.D. Greek scientist and philosopher Ptolemy. This view of the world became a part of Catholic theology through the work of Thomas Aquinas. According to this model, Earth was the center of the universe, the motion of heavenly bodies was perfect circular motion, and those heavenly bodies were immune to change, obeying different laws of motion than those of Earth. There were, then, two separate realms—the higher worlds of the heavens and the lower world of the Earth. The Scientific Revolution shattered this model.

Roman Catholicism argued that authority rested with Scripture, tradition, and the institutionalized church. The Reformation countered that authority resided only in Scripture. Luther's cry, "*Sola Scriptura*," meant a clear rejection of the dogma of Catholicism as empty and erroneous, including the detailed arguments of the Scholastics. For many this rejection included speculations about science. The shift from the institutional church to the Bible as the source of religious authority played a crucial role in advancing the acceptance of new scientific ideas.

In addition, Protestants challenged the Western world to reject the philosophical speculations of Catholic theology that was developed apart from Scripture. Aristotle's philosophy, which had so strongly influenced Aquinas, led Catholicism down the road to vain and idle conjectures (e.g., the worship of Mary, purgatory, the mass). The natural operation of human reason, unchecked by the Bible, could only lead to error and vanity. That, Protestants claimed, was precisely what had happened to Catholic theology. Thinkers of the seventeenth century agreed and rejected along with theology the Catholic speculations about science.

Finally, Protestant affirmations about the sovereignty of God, especially in the dynamic of salvation, laid the groundwork for seventeenth-century thinking about science. Both Luther and Calvin maintained the absolute sovereignty and rule of God over His creation. The extent of human depravity was so immense that only God's active intervention by His grace could save a person. Hence, the doctrines of election and predestination.

God's sovereignty, with His active and dynamic involvement, meant no intermediaries, whether it was in salvation or in the natural world. Catholicism viewed the world as a hierarchy, with many intermediaries between God and the physical world. Not so with Protestantism. Luther and Calvin saw only Christ as an intermediary; the church as go-between had no biblical support. Similarly, God acted directly in nature. To study nature was to study God at work. Protestantism and the new science both held that truth came from studying God's Word and God's world.

A NEW MODEL FOR THE PHYSICAL WORLD

As the Reformation challenged Catholic assumptions, sixteenth-century scientists challenged natural assumptions. They all worked from a Christian worldview and did not see their work as threatening Christianity. Each believed that studying God's world proved that God was a God of order, purpose, and design. Through their study they likewise dismantled the old Aristotelian model and formulated a new model for the universe.

Modern science was born as philosophers asked new questions about how humans think and gain knowledge. An English philosopher, Francis Bacon (1561–1626), proposed a new method for arriving at knowledge and truth. That method involved the systematic recording of facts, which then led to tentative hypotheses that were tested by experiments. The end result of this inductive method was universal principles and scientific laws.

Even more significant was a French philosopher, Rene Descartes (1596–1650), who began his method with doubting everything, except that he was doubting. Since he doubted, he therefore existed: "I think, therefore, I am" (Discourse on Method, 120). Secondly, he believed that he could prove the existence of God. He found in his mind the idea of a "more perfect being." This idea, he concluded, could only have been placed there by God. Therefore, humans possess certain innate ideas that form the building blocks of understanding and knowledge. These innate ideas are sourced in God. Through the process of reason, Descartes further concluded, humans built upon these clear and distinct precepts and arrived at universal principles. This is the method of deduction.

In contrast to Descartes's concept of innate ideas was the empiricism of John Locke (1632–1704). He rejected Descartes's innate ideas and argued instead that knowledge is derived from experience. How does this view affect matters of faith? Locke argued that faith is an assent to knowledge derived from revelation rather than reason. Therefore, its knowledge is never certain, only probable. In 1695 Locke published The Reasonableness of Christianity, in which he claimed that Christianity is the most reasonable of faiths. The essence of the Christian faith is belief in God's existence and personal faith in Jesus as Messiah. But these truths are probable truths, not certain truths, he believed. Locke argued that one must separate probable judgments of faith from the certainty of empirical reason. Conduct and toleration of other beliefs are more important than the narrowness of Christian doctrine. The devastating implications of Locke's thinking for Christianity are obvious.

It was in the scientific discipline of astronomy that experimentation, observation, and mathematical reasoning found their union. Copernicus (1473–1543), in his Concerning the Revolution of Heavenly Spheres, argued that Earth revolved around the sun every twenty-four hours, thereby challenging the Earth-centered universe of Aristotle and Aquinas. Johannes Kepler (1571–1630) gave mathematical proof to Copernicus's theory and discovered that the planets move in an ellipse, not the perfect circle of Aristotle. Galileo Galilei (1564–1642), using the newly invented telescope, discovered mountains on the moon, observed sunspots, and discovered a moon of Jupiter. All of these discoveries demonstrated that not all heavenly bodies orbit Earth and that change is part of the heavens too.

The central figure of the Scientific Revolution, however, was Isaac Newton (1642–1727). Newton synthesized Kepler and Galileo by asserting that one all-embracing principle—the law of gravity— explained motion in the universe. This law applied to both Earth and the heavens. Newton thus proposed order, consistency, and uniformity throughout the universe. When it came to God's natural laws, there were no distinctions between heaven and Earth. So profound was Newton's work that Alexander Pope wrote in his *Epitaph. Intended for Sir Isaac Newton, In Westminster Abbey* (1730):

> *Nature and Nature's Laws lay hid in Night;*
> *God said, "Let Newton be," and All was* Light.[1]

THE REACTION OF QUAKERISM, GERMAN PIETISM, AND METHODISM

The Protestantism of the seventeenth century had become cold, impersonal, and, for some, stifling. Many reform movements developed in response. One was Quakerism. Founded in England by George Fox (1624–1691), Quakerism argued that it had discovered the true meaning of faith and Christianity. Hymns, orders of worship, sermons, sacraments, creeds, and ministers were all human hindrances to the true freedom of Christianity, which is found in the Spirit. Fox believed that a seed existed in all humans, called the "inner light," that each person must follow to find God. This inner light is the key to recognizing and accepting the presence of God and understanding His Word.

Fox's followers became known as "friends," and because of the trembling that often accompanied their worship, others referred to them as "Quakers." Because Quakers rejected worship structure of any kind, their worship took place in silence. When the Spirit moved them, men and women had the freedom to speak and pray aloud. In an age of conformity, structure, and orthodoxy, Quakerism developed as an expression of radical individualism. Persecuted intensely, many Quakers fled England for the freedom of the colonies, especially Pennsylvania.

Another important response to the formalism of mature Protestantism was German Pietism. *The Oxford Dictionary of the Christian*

Church (p. 1089) defines Pietism as "a seventeenth-century movement in the German Church which had as its purpose the infusion of new life into the official Protestantism of its time." German Pietists such as John Arndt (1555–1621), Philipp Spener (1635–1705), August Francke (1663–1727), and Nicholas von Zinzendorf (1700–1760) revived German Lutheranism. They believed that Christians should meet in small house meetings to gain a better understanding of the Bible. The laity, not only professional ministers, should be allowed to exercise their spiritual priesthood. Although they believed in the importance of the mind, Pietists placed emphasis on the practical side of Christianity, highlighting personal holiness. Religious controversies needed to be handled with a spirit of love. Finally, Pietists believed that the pulpit should be for instructing, edifying, and inspiring believers, not for learned lectures on cryptic points of doctrine.

Pietism breathed new life into staid and stiff European Christianity and also influenced the development of American Christianity and modern missions (see chapters 10 and 11). But its influence on the experiential nature of Christianity often was at the expense of doctrine. Later developments in European Christianity would demonstrate the danger of this emphasis.

Another response to cold and detached seventeenth-century Christianity was Methodism. Founded by John Wesley (1703–1791), Methodism grew out of the Anglican church. A member of the Holy Club at Oxford University, Wesley struggled with personal holiness. He pastored and even served as a missionary in the new colony of Georgia. But it was not until he came into contact with the Pietistic Moravians that he met his Lord. On May 24, 1738, at a meeting of Moravians on Aldersgate Street in London, Wesley trusted Christ as his Savior.

Wesley devoted the rest of his life to preaching the Gospel. He traveled all over England, especially to the new industrial centers, where Methodism grew rapidly. He also utilized women and lay preachers to spread the message of salvation. Similar strategies brought Methodism to the American frontier, where it spread quickly. Methodism brought new life to English Christianity.

With the Scientific Revolution, the old model of the universe was dead. A new one had dawned. Earth was one of many planets that orbited the sun and not the center of the universe. Universal laws of physics applied to all planets and to all heavenly bodies. The seventeenth century increasingly viewed the universe as a machine operating according to physical laws that could be discovered and understood by reason and expressed mathematically. The question now was, what is the role of God? Did the Reformation view of Him as the Creator and Sovereign of the world still hold? If the physical laws of the universe were discoverable through reason, could reason yield a science of man as well as physics? Is truth something discovered or revealed? These were some of the questions the Scientific Revolution raised and with which Quakerism, Pietism, and Methodism struggled. But their answers were different from the Enlightenment's answers, the subject of the next chapter.

FOR FURTHER DISCUSSION

1. Briefly explain the model of the universe Aristotle defended. What Roman Catholic theologian made Aristotle's views part of Catholic theology?

2. Explain how the Reformation helped prepare the way for the Scientific Revolution.

3. Show the role each played in undermining the old model of the physical universe:

   a.   Bacon—
   b.   Descartes—
   c.   Copernicus—
   d.   Kepler—
   e.   Galileo—
   f.   Newton—

4. What were the key elements in the new worldview of the Scientific Revolution?

THE CHURCH, THE ENLIGHTENMENT, AND THEOLOGICAL LIBERALISM

The Enlightenment represents man's emergence from a self-inflicted state of minority. . . . Have the courage to make use of your own understanding is the watchword of the Enlightenment.

IMMANUEL KANT, 1793

The eighteenth-century Enlightenment was a movement of ideas that sought to release humanity from error and prejudice and to achieve truth, which in turn would produce freedom. Many Enlightenment thinkers targeted religion, for they saw it as embodying the error and prejudice they loathed. Specifically, they regarded Christianity and all other religions as irrational and inappropriate in a scientific age. The Enlightenment sought rational explanations for all of reality; religion was no exception.

THE ENLIGHTENMENT

Where the Scientific Revolution showed the order and rationality of the universe and discovered the laws governing the physical universe, the Enlightenment desired to examine human institutions to find the same kind of order and consistency and to posit laws that governed society. In short, they sought a science of man that would free him from all bondage. Some of the principal thinkers of the Enlightenment were Voltaire (1694–1778), Jean Jacques Rousseau (1712–1778), Denis Diderot (1713–1784), and David Hume (1711–1776).

At bottom, Enlightenment thinkers were critical of everything. The method of the critic was the engine driving their analysis of society's institutions, including the church, the law, and even government. One French philosopher said, "all things must be examined, debated, investigated, without exception and without regard for anyone's feelings" (Gay, 1:128). With confidence in human reason and science, the Enlightenment championed the destruction of all barriers to human freedom and autonomy.

In addition, the eighteenth century was a period of skepticism, with many doubting the certainty of knowing absolute, universal truths. David Hume, the Scottish philosopher, epitomized this skeptical commitment. Central to Hume's position was the idea that no generalization about experience is ever rationally justified. As Norman Geisler has shown, Hume maintained that no proposition about experience is necessary, for one can easily imagine a world where the proposition would be false. As a generalization about reality, "the sun will rise tomorrow" is not necessary, for we can conceive of a world like ours where the sun will not rise tomorrow. For Hume, probability does not lead to certainty. Therefore, he denied the certainty of cause-effect relationships, attacked arguments for the existence of God, and authored a blistering attack on a belief in miracles.

John Locke (1632–1704) embodied the devotion to empiricism, a decisive characteristic of the Enlightenment. For Locke, humans were born with no sense of right or wrong or of any innate truths. Instead, the human mind is like a blank slate that throughout life is filled with data coming from the senses. Mysteries and doctrines of Christianity that could not be empirically proven were distrusted and often rejected. Following Locke, many Enlightenment thinkers repudiated all religion, including Christianity, as superstitious. They thought that religion needed to be replaced with a rational system of ethics.

Most of the Enlightenment thinkers, however, were not atheists; instead, many were deists. A philosophy difficult to summarize, deism proclaimed that one God created the world to operate on perfect natural law. But He no longer intervened in its present functioning, either by revelation or miracle. Thus deists rejected the Bible, gospel miracles, the Incarnation, and the Resurrection. Deism is a system in which God is an absentee landlord who has no involvement with His physical creation. He made the perfect clock and then left.

Voltaire's deism is perhaps most representative. He wrote: "I believe in God; not the God of the mystics but the God of nature, the great geometrician, the architect of the Universe, the prime mover, unalterable, transcendent, everlasting. . . . I shall always be convinced that a watch proves a watch-maker and that a universe proves a God" (Redman, 196). Voltaire rejected the special revelation of God in the Bible but embraced the God who created the physical universe. The deist's God was their Creator, but He was not their Savior!

The Enlightenment had a devastating effect on Christianity. First, because of Locke's empiricism, the Enlightenment affirmed the basic goodness of man. There was no doctrine of innate evil or original sin. Second, for the Enlightenment the human environment was determinative in shaping character and intelligence. Education was crucial in sharpening the senses, pursuing science, and changing human outlook and prejudice. It was the key to transforming people. Third, the Enlightenment was a thoroughly man-centered movement. Belief in the basic goodness of man held that under the proper circumstances, there was really nothing humans could not achieve.

Near the end of the eighteenth century, the doctrine of progress characterized the Enlightenment mind. Man was on an escalator, and nothing hindered him from going all the way to the top. Moral, spiritual, and technological progress seemed inevitable. Finally, the Enlightenment raised serious questions about the need for God. But with the emphasis on reason and science, God seemed irrelevant and unnecessary. With the rejection of objective revelation and skepticism about the supernatural, how can we know much about Him at all? This redefining of God laid the groundwork for the theological liberalism of the nineteenth century.

The Enlightenment also altered the connection between faith and reason for its followers. Near the end of the Enlightenment, Immanuel Kant (1724–1804) wrote several books attacking the traditional proofs for the existence of God. For Kant, the realm of knowledge was divided into two fundamentally separate domains, one that is knowable (the phenomena) and one that is not knowable (the *noumena*). Questions about God, immortality, and freedom of the human fell into the second category, and no empirical verification was thought possible. Kant therefore blocked the road to a knowledge of God through reason. One could not know God, he claimed, for there was no way to verify His existence rationally.

For Kant, then, what was religion? Religion was mostly human-centered in its orientation and grounded in a sense of duty and obligation. To Kant, religion was not an objective set of beliefs rooted in God's revelation to man. Instead, one lived *as if* God existed and was accountable to Him. Personal religion was a set of ethics, not propositional theology. As theologian Dr. Norman Geisler has remarked, "Kant kicked God out the front door and ran around and let Him in the back door" (from a lecture at Grace University). According to Kant, you do not know for certain that God exists, but you live as if He does!

THE ENLIGHTENMENT AND THEOLOGICAL LIBERALISM

As Kant blocked the road to God through reason for many, the only road left was the interior life, the realm of subjective experience. Friedrich Schleiermacher (1768–1834), the founder of modern theological liberalism, wrote in *The Christian Faith* (p. 125), "You reject the dogmas and propositions of religion. . . . Religion does not need them; it is only human reflection on the content of our religious feelings or affections. . . . Do you say that you cannot accept miracles, revelation, inspiration? You are right; we are children no longer; the time for fairytales is past." To Schleiermacher, religion was not knowledge as orthodox Christianity believed; nor was it a system of ethics as Kant implied. Rather, it was a "feeling" of dependence on God.

For Schleiermacher, "the feeling of absolute dependence" (*The Christian Faith*, 131) constituted the essence of religion. He believed Jesus was a man who exhibited such God-conscious dependence. Christ's work on the cross served as a model of self-denying love for us to emulate in all ways. Gone was any affirmation of Christ's deity, His substitutionary atonement, or propositional revelation from God.

If Christianity was reduced to feeling and Jesus was merely a suffering man, then the question for Enlightenment thinkers became, can we trust the New Testament accounts of Jesus? David Strauss's (1808–1874) book, *The Life of Jesus*, interjected the word *myth* into the discussion about the gospel accounts. He argued that the supernatural elements in the Gospels were not trustworthy. Miracles—for example, the Resurrection—were reflections by New Testament writers on Jesus' life. The Gospels were not history, said Strauss: "The life of Jesus was 'mythically' rewritten in order that writers might express their awareness of the significance of Jesus" (*The Life of Jesus*, 778).

If the New Testament then contains myth, what is the distinctive nature of Christianity? Theological liberalism reduced the Christian faith to righteous behavior grounded in the ethic of love. Albrecht Ritschl (1822–1889) maintained that the man Jesus Christ embodied this ethic. For Ritschl, the center of Jesus' teaching was the kingdom of God and its ethics, "the organization of humanity through action based on love" (Ritschl, 1:13). Furthermore, Adolf von Harnack (1851–1930), in his groundbreaking book *What is Christianity?*, asserted that the essence of the Christian faith was "the fatherhood of God and the brotherhood of man." To Harnack, Christianity was the commandment of love. To make the theology of Jesus more important than the work of Jesus was a "great departure from what Jesus thought and enjoined" (Fletcher, 62-63). To Harnack, the history of doctrine was the movement from the teachings of Jesus to the teachings about Jesus.

Was Christianity unique? Not to liberal theology. Between 1880 and 1920, in what was called the History of Religions School in Germany, Christianity was regarded as a human religion like all others that needed to be studied historically. Jesus was a historical figure but not the one pictured in the New Testament. In addition, the liberals said that Paul, influenced by Greek Gnosticism, probably distorted what Jesus taught. There was, then, no continuity between the Old Testament and the New Testament. For most of the leaders of this school, the Old Testament had little influence in shaping Christianity.

Liberal theology next began a quest for the historical Jesus. Its theologians asked, since we cannot trust the New Testament, what is the ground on which we can build our understanding of Jesus? Rudolf Bultmann (1884–1976) called for the "demythologizing" of the Gospels, the peeling off of the husks, to find the kernel of truth. That Jesus existed, Bultmann argued, is about all that can be claimed as certain. The anti-supernaturalism of the Enlightenment reached its peak with Bultmann.

One major German theologian, Karl Barth (1886–1968), turned away from theological liberalism. Trained in this school of theology, Barth struggled in the pastorate. He concluded that he had nothing to offer his people. He abandoned much of liberal theology and espoused a more orthodox, reformed interpretation of Christianity. He affirmed the utter transcendence of God and the chasm that existed between God and man. Only Jesus, the revelation of God, bridged that chasm, he argued. The Bible, then, is the revelation of God because it gives a witness to

Jesus. Man meets God in a "crisis" when the Word of God "becomes" real to man. It is this crisis experience that formed one of the distinctives of Barth's neo-orthodoxy. In the end his interpretation satisfied very few people.

The antisupernaturalism of the Enlightenment produced the theological liberalism of the nineteenth and twentieth centuries. Kant separated faith and reason, declared man self-reliant, and claimed that absolute truths about God were unknowable. Faith for many now had no foundation. In attempting to find a new underpinning, theological liberalism cut all ties to the Bible as historical and trustworthy. Christianity became an ethical system, not all that different from other religions. But that is not the only story. Despite liberalism's major inroads into Christianity, God's program of redemption continued with the eruption of the modern missions movement throughout the world—the subject of the next chapter.

For Further Discussion

1. Why can we say that the Enlightenment was an attack on organized religion, especially on Christianity?
2. What was deism?
3. How did the Enlightenment challenge some of Christianity's teachings?
4. Explain Immanual Kant's view on the relationship between faith and reason. Why was this so harmful to Christianity?
5. Theological liberalism was a child of the Enlightenment. Show how each of the following built on the foundation of the Enlightenment:
   Friedrich Schleiermacher—
   Albrecht Ritschl—
   Adolf von Harnack—
   Rudolf Bultmann—
6. In what ways did Karl Barth disagree with liberalism?

THE CHURCH AND MODERN MISSIONS

Expect great things from God;
attempt great things for God.

WILLIAM CAREY

The Great Commission of Jesus Christ defines the church's mission. But church history demonstrates that the church has not always taken that mission seriously. Although the ancient and early medieval church took the Gospel to the Germanic tribes, the medieval church neglected missions for centuries. Fighting for survival, the Reformation church also lacked missionary zeal. During the last two hundred years, a passion for reaching the world for Christ has enriched the modern church. This is especially true of the nineteenth century, which has been called the "Great Century of Missions." That missionary passion produced the first truly universal church, in which all races and nations had a part. This is the story of that passion.

ROOTS OF THE MODERN MISSIONS MOVEMENT

The roots of the modern missions movement reach back to the revivals of the eighteenth century (see next chapter). These movements of God's Spirit gave the fervor and energy so necessary for cross-cultural ministry. But other factors provided a fuller context. The voyages of discovery that opened the western hemisphere raised theological questions about where the people of this hemisphere came from and whether they were redeemable. The trading companies that settled North America demanded a spiritual emphasis in their charters. Also the Catholic church, especially the Jesuits, had modeled missionary activity for several centuries.

These developments coincided with the rise of industrial capitalism in Europe and the United States. As capitalism spread, the need for raw materials and markets for the finished products spawned a need for conquest of the remaining continents—Africa and Asia. The major European powers—France, England, and the Netherlands—competed to plant colonies on those continents. The nineteenth century was thus a century of imperialism. Most Europeans, including Protestant Christians, looked at imperialist activity as taking the benefits of capitalism, democracy, and Christianity to the needy world. Author Rudyard Kipling called this the "White Man's Burden." Trade, hospitals, roads, and industrial development did come to these continents, but so did racism and exploitation.

WILLIAM CAREY—"THE FATHER OF MODERN MISSIONS"

As colonists expanded into Africa and Asia, they took the Gospel with them. Early missionary societies were the sending agencies—the Danish-Halle Mission (1704), the Scottish Society for Propagating Christian Knowledge (1707), and Moravian Missions (1732). All of these societies owed their existence to the Pietistic revivals of the eighteenth century. But it was William Carey (1761–1834), founder of the Particular Baptist Society for Propagating the Gospel Among the Heathen, who became "the father of modern missions."

As a teacher, Carey was captivated by the stories of Captain Cook's discoveries in the Pacific. The intersection of these stories and his Baptist faith produced a deep conviction that the church had an obligation to proclaim the news of Jesus Christ to the unreached peoples of the world. He joined with others of a like mind and formed the Particular Baptist Society. In 1793 he and his family went to Calcutta, India. The work was difficult but fruitful, and his enthusiasm and intensity did much to cause others to venture out to other lands. His famous dictum, "Expect great things from God; attempt great things for God," still inspires people today.

Carey's ministry in India provided the model for modern missions. First, it depended on donations from private individuals and churches. Second, Carey regularly communicated with home churches and individuals, which generated increased interest in missions. Third, he made the Bible available to the Indian population. With an innate gift for learning languages, Carey translated the Bible, or parts of it, into thirty-five different languages. Fourth, in addition to planting churches, Carey's work and that of his followers promoted medical help and education as a part of the ministry. Finally, the gospel message had social and cultural implications. Carey personally toiled to end the burning of widows on their husbands' funeral pyres. Others insisted that India's caste system was wrong. Members of India's lowest caste, the Untouchables, and Indian women found Christianity personally liberating.

Others followed in Carey's path. Adoniram Judson (1788–1850), a Baptist missionary from America, did pioneer work in Burma very similar to Carey's. A group of English Congregationalists, among them David Livingstone and Robert Moffat, founded the London Missionary Society (1795), which did pioneer work in southern Africa.

MISSIONS IN EARLY AMERICA

The Haystack Prayer Meeting launched the missionary movement in America. In 1806 students at Williams College in Massachusetts took refuge from a thunderstorm under a haystack for their prayer meeting. Their motto was, "We can do it if we will." The resulting society eventually became known as the American Board of Commissioners for Foreign Missions (1810). By the end of the Civil War, fifteen mission boards serviced the major denominations of America.

THE EXAMPLE OF J. HUDSON TAYLOR

The modern missions movement, however, found its greatest power and influence in the faith missions movement, founded by J. Hudson Taylor (1832–1905). Born in England, Taylor underwent a deep spiritual conversion at the age of seventeen. He felt a distinct call to the nearly closed empire of China, where he began his ministry in 1854. Forced to return to England due to ill health, he devoted himself to founding and then leading the China Inland Mission (CIM). Strongly interdenominational and dependent on God for support, CIM became the vanguard for spiritual awakening in China. Taylor went back to China where he meticulously led the opening of each province to the Gospel. By 1895 there were 641 CIM missionaries in China. Through his writings and world speaking tours, Taylor's influence extended far beyond China. Today the faith missions movement he founded includes at least fifteen thousand missionaries representing more than seventy-five different faith missions.

Other faith missions that followed Taylor's model included the Christian and Missionary Alliance founded by A. B. Simpson in 1887, the Evangelical Alliance Mission founded by Fredrik Franson in 1890, and the African Inland Mission founded by Peter Cameron Scott in 1895. Through the first several decades of the twentieth century, dozens more would be founded.

THE CONTRIBUTIONS OF MODERN MISSIONS

The achievements of the modern missionary enterprise have been staggering. First, literally millions of people have found eternal life. Every ethnic, racial, and language group is now represented in the universal church of Jesus Christ. Second, national churches, with scores of local churches, now exist in virtually every nation of the world. Third, mission agencies planted thousands of educational institutions throughout the world. Fourth, Christianity became a liberating force for women and other underprivileged groups in the native cultures. The social and ethical implications of the Christian faith have often had profound, transforming effects on the native culture. Fifth, Christian mission agencies usually built medical facilities, including large hospitals, to care for the medical needs of the native population. Finally, the modern missionary movement has made the Bible available in hundreds of languages throughout the world. The Wycliffe Bible Translators, founded in 1934, is the best example of this extraordinary effort.

The modern missionary endeavor has literally changed the world.[1] North America has provided the majority of missionaries for this movement, and the revivals that have dotted American history provided the catalyst for this army of change-agents.

FOR FURTHER DISCUSSION

1. What were some of the factors that explain why modern missions exploded in the nineteenth century?
2. Summarize the importance of William Carey.
3. Summarize the importance of Hudson Taylor to faith missions.
4. List the positive effects that modern missions has had on the church and the world.

The Growth of the Gospel

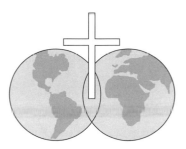

GOD IS BUILDING HIS CHURCH—RAPIDLY

Across the centuries, Bible-believing Christians have become an ever-larger proportion of the world population. In A.D. 1430, only one person in one hundred was a Bible-believing Christian. Today, one in nine is. This means 600 million out of 5.7 billion people in the world are Bible-believing Christians. This huge body of believers is growing at a rate of *more than three times* that of the world population!

MILESTONE DATES IN THE GROWTH OF TRUE CHRISTIANITY

—At the dates indicated, a comparison of
1) the number of Bible-believing Christians and
2) the total number of people in the world:

One per hundred **(1%)** by	**A.D. 1430**	(One to **99** after **1430** years)
Two per hundred **(2%)** by	**A.D. 1790**	(One to **49** after **360** years)
Three per hundred **(3%)** by	**A.D. 1940**	(One to **32** after **150** years)
Four per hundred **(4%)** by	**A.D. 1960**	(One to **24** after **20** years)
Five per hundred **(5%)** by	**A.D. 1970**	(One to **19** after **10** years)
Six per hundred **(6%)** by	**A.D. 1980**	(One to **16** after **10** years)
Seven per hundred **(7%)** by	**A.D. 1983**	(One to **13** after **3** years)
Eight per hundred **(8%)** by	**A.D. 1986**	(One to **11** after **3** years)
Nine per hundred **(9%)** by	**A.D. 1989**	(One to **10** after **3** years)
Ten per hundred **(10%)** by	**A.D. 1993**	(One to **9** after **4** years)
Eleven per hundred **(11%)** by	**A.D. 1995**	(One to **8** after **2** years)

"Bible-believing Christian" refers to those people who read, believe, and obey the Bible whether or not they are yet as active as they ought to be in helping out with world evangelization.

WHERE DO THESE AMAZING NUMBERS COME FROM?

Major milestone dates down through history were supplied by the Lausanne Statistics Task Force, headed by David Barrett, Ph.D., author of the *World Christian Encyclopedia*. The intermediate values here were then calculated (exponentially) for these specific milestone dates. From the January-February, 1996 edition of *Mission Frontiers*, The Bulletin of the U.S. Center for World Mission, Pasadena, California. Used by permission.

THE CHURCH AND REVIVALS IN AMERICA

The whole theory of revivals is involved in these two facts;
viz., that the influence of the Holy Spirit is concerned in
every instance of sound conversion, and that this influence
is granted in more copious measure and in greater power
at some times than at others. When these facts concur,
there is revival of religion.

JOEL HAWES, 1871

Because revivals have been so frequent in America, one could easily study American history solely from their perspective. Each century has seen at least one period of renewal that molded the nation's development. The purpose of this chapter is to reconstruct the decisive impact revivals have had on the development of American society.

Undeniably, American civilization of the seventeenth century was tied almost exclusively to the Protestant Reformation. The Pilgrims and Puritans who settled New England were devout Calvinists. Baptistic groups came to Rhode Island and the middle colonies. Presbyterians established churches in both the middle and southern colonies. The Anglican church was central to the planting of Virginia, the Carolinas, Georgia, and New York. Lutherans also settled in the middle colonies. The only exception to Protestant dominance was Maryland, a quasi-Catholic colony, and Pennsylvania, a Quaker colony that practiced remarkable religious tolerance.

THE FIRST GREAT AWAKENING

By the eighteenth century, it was clear that the church needed renewal. There was an acute shortage of spiritual leadership in the churches, and few opportunities for adequate ministerial training existed in America. In addition, the reordering of the political relationships with the British Empire caused an unsettledness among many colonials. Finally, the second and third generations that now inhabited the American colonies had lost the original vision that had sent their forefathers to the New World. God in His grace, therefore, sent a revival to His church. That revival is usually called the First Great Awakening.

The move of God apparently began in the 1720s among the Dutch Reformed churches in the colony of New Jersey. A Dutchman named Theodore Frelinghuysen (1691–1748) came to minister there and preached moral purity and the need for a profound, not perfunctory, commitment to Christ. The churches began to grow in numbers, and members deepened in piety. Frelinghuysen found friends of like mind in the Tennent family, committed Presbyterians who believed that proper theological training was the key to bringing life to dead churches. William Tennent, Sr., (1673–1746) began to train young men for pastoral ministry in a school that became known as the Log College in the 1730s. The "graduates" of that college fanned out across the middle and southern colonies with the Gospel. They laid the groundwork for spiritual renewal in America.

Jonathan Edwards (1703–1758) gave pivotal leadership to the revival in New England. At seventeen Edwards graduated from Yale and took a pastorate in Northampton in 1727, where he served until 1750. His famous 1741 sermon, "Sinners in the Hands of an Angry God," epitomized the power of words in an age when sermons were usually read in a monotone voice. Edwards's preaching power contributed to the revival that swept through the entire Connecticut River valley. He also made a powerful defense of the emotionalism that often accompanied revivals, seeing this as evidence of the sovereign God at work. His involvement with George Whitefield (1714–1770) deepened the New England awakening.

As the best-known Protestant of the eighteenth century, George Whitefield gave an exceptional degree of unity to the colonial revival. A friend of John and Charles Wesley, Whitefield was a member of the Holy Club at Oxford University in the 1720s and 1730s. He made seven tours of the colonies, preaching up and down the coast of America. His impact on the New England revival was especially marked. It was his preaching style that appealed to the common American colonial. He used plain language that was easy to understand, and he contributed immensely to the more democratic and popular style of Christianity that was developing in late colonial America.

Largely through the leadership of Isaac Backus (1724–1806), New England Baptists grew and became institutionalized in the culture. In addition to championing adult baptism, Baptists stood for the separation of church and state; they resisted the traditional New England support of the churches by the government. The need for trained leaders led to the founding of a Baptist College in Rhode Island in 1764, later known as Brown University.

The Baptist work in the southern colonies was led by Shubal Stearns (1706–1771) and Daniel Marshall (1706–1784), who together founded a Baptist Association of churches at Sandy Creek, North Carolina, in 1755. Through this Association, Baptist churches burst across the South. The typical Baptist preacher was not well-educated, instead, he was often a farmer who preached on Sunday to his small country church. Such a Baptist model was appealing to the rural South and largely explains Baptist growth.

Lastly, the Methodist church, under the leadership of Devereaux Jarrett (1743–1801), gained strength in Virginia and North Carolina and laid the groundwork for the eruption of growth that would follow under Francis Asbury. Like the Baptists, Methodists appealed to the poor and uneducated of the South. Methodist ministers, with their simple gospel message, were often willing to go where the educated clergy would not.

The impact of the First Great Awakening on American civilization was staggering. Because of theological controversy generated by the revivals, Presbyterians and Congregationalists split. Two new denominations gained a strong foothold in America—the Baptists and the Methodists. Further, a new zeal and energy characterized American churches. New converts and new churches dotted the evangelical landscape of America. Missionary work among the slaves and the Indians resulted. David Brainerd (1718–1747) endured great hardships to take the Gospel to the Seneca and Delaware Indians. Evangelists Samuel Davies (1723–1761) and George Whitefield both ministered to slaves during this period. The Awakening built important bridges to Native Americans and African-Americans.

The Awakening, as the first truly national event, likewise had powerful cultural implications for the new nation. Either through his preaching or his writing, George Whitefield touched virtually every American. His preaching tours throughout the colonies gave a measure of cultural unity unlike anything else at that time. This linkage often transcended ethnic barriers and provided a growing distrust of England and the Anglican church. Finally, the revivals resulted in a new form of spiritual leadership in the colonies. Gone were the days when only a highly educated clergy had legitimacy. Now the itinerant minister, often without formal education, preached that a person's relationship with God was more important than status or social standing. In many ways, the Awakening helped foster a growing commitment to democratic-republican ideals. That is why religious words such as *liberty* and *virtue* had strong social/political connotations as well.

THE SECOND GREAT AWAKENING

The American Revolution (1776–1783) profoundly changed American society. Not only did the colonies become an independent country—the United States of America—but the churches of America played a vital role in supporting the independence cause and giving leadership to it. The political ideology of the Revolution, called Republicanism, shared common tenets with Protestant Christianity. Both viewed history as a struggle between good and evil, with America clearly on the side of the good. Both viewed power and tyranny as the enemy of liberty. America, each argued, symbolized liberty and Britain, tyranny. Therefore, preachers of Congregational, Baptist, and Presbyterian congregations openly supported the independence cause as the cause of Christ and His kingdom.

However, with the nation established and the new Constitution written, a growing secularism took hold in America. In fact, through pamphlets and books, the deism that had fueled Enlightenment thinking filtered down to the masses. In addition, the new territories west of the Appalachian Mountains were generally devoid of any gospel witness. Economically, the nation faced hard times, even coming close to defaulting on its debts. Prices for staples soared, a plague of worms destroyed the corn and fruit crops, and diseases, including smallpox, ravaged the population. In many ways a crisis mentality characterized the nation. But from about 1790 to 1810, a broad-based revival swept across the new nation. It was the most significant revival in American history.

The southwestern phase of the revival began from the desire of one man to reach the frontier for Christ. James McGready (1758–1817) pastored three small churches in rural Logan County, Kentucky. Impressed by the writings of Jonathan Edwards, he led his people in a monthly fast and weekly prayer meetings for revival. Once a year he brought all the churches together on a mountainside to observe the Lord's Table. An outpouring of the Spirit at one of these gatherings drew many people from other churches. That Communion service birthed the first camp meeting, the form revival mainly took on the frontier. Camp meetings offered days and often weeks of gatherings where Presbyterian, Baptist, and Methodist preachers proclaimed the Gospel to eager listeners. In addition, Methodist circuit riders and Baptist lay preachers spread the Gospel throughout the South and the West, transforming the denominational landscape and spiritual climate of these regions.

The eastern phase of the Awakening centered on the college campuses. Timothy Dwight (1752–1817), newly appointed president of Yale, led a revival on that campus that brought hundreds to Christ. These students in turn carried revival throughout New England, New York, and the West. Similar developments occurred at the southern Presbyterian college of Hampden-Sydney.

Although the First Great Awakening dramatically affected the colonies, the Second Awakening had a more lasting effect on American life. First, Methodists, Baptists, and the newly formed Disciples of Christ spearheaded the revival, leaving the Congregationalists, Presbyterians, and Anglicans far behind. Methodists, Baptists, and the Disciples went on to dominate American Protestantism for decades.

Second, the Awakening produced durable institutions that impacted American culture well into the twentieth century. Institutions such as the American Bible Society (1816), the American Sunday School Union (1824), the American Tract Society (1825), the American Society for the Promotion of Temperance (1826), and numerous others owed their reform vision to the transforming zeal of the Second Awakening.

Finally, the Awakening represented a fundamental shift in American theology. Where the Puritans of the seventeenth century focused on a God-centered theology that stressed man's inability to save himself, the early nineteenth century embraced a man-centered theology that emphasized the free will and responsibility of man in salvation. In many ways, the Second Awakening marked the death knell of Calvinism as a major force in American religious life.

CHARLES GRANDISON FINNEY

This shift away from a God-centered theology accelerated with the revivalistic and evangelistic preaching of Charles Finney (1792–1875).

Finney trusted Christ in 1821 and changed his vocation from lawyer to minister. Throughout the remainder of the 1820s and into the 1830s, Finney conducted revival meetings in key Northern cities. These ventures gained him national prominence. In addition, some of his converts founded key reform movements, especially those dedicated to the abolition of slavery.

Charles Finney radically altered the direction of American Christianity. First, he introduced many "new measures"[1] into American evangelism. Because he believed so strongly in human free will, he thought that the evangelist, if he followed the proper methods, could reap a harvest of converts. Therefore, he utilized the protracted meeting; the anxious bench for repentant sinners; long, emotional prayers; and organized choirs—all designed to break the stubborn will of the prospective convert.

Second, Finney advocated a strong postmillennialism in his theology. He believed that the church, through its efforts at reforming society, could usher in the kingdom of God now! The kingdom could come in three years, he often said.

Finally, Finney's man-centered theology led him to advocate a perfectionism when it came to sanctification. Finney taught that some Christians could reach a permanent sanctified state in which they do not knowingly sin. He truly believed that Christians who were entirely sanctified could bring about a thorough reform of society so that the kingdom of God would come to America. Such optimism dovetailed perfectly with the individualism and self-sufficiency of the new nation.

THE LAYMAN'S PRAYER REVIVAL OF 1858

One of the most remarkable American revivals took place in 1858. Lacking any one leader, this renewal was thoroughly lay-oriented and took place largely in the cities. Praying, not preaching, sparked the movement that started in a noonday prayer meeting in New York. Soon interdenominational prayer meetings started up in most of the major cities of the North, with more than two thousand people jamming Chicago's daily prayer meeting at the Metropolitan Theater. The revival then spread to rural areas, including the South, to Europe, especially England, and even to Australia. The awakening helped establish the historical context for Moody, the Salvation Army, and the rise of the faith missions movement, all after the Civil War.

D. L. MOODY

D. L. Moody (1837–1899) and Billy Sunday both built their ministries on the "new measures" foundation of Charles Finney. Each represented the triumph of mass evangelism in Protestant America. Increasingly, as mass production triumphed in business, the same techniques crossed over into evangelism.

Born in Northfield, Massachusetts, Dwight Lyman Moody was a successful shoe salesman in both Boston and Chicago. Converted in his late teens, Moody started a Sunday school in the Chicago slums in 1858 and by 1866 was president of the Chicago YMCA. For Moody there was no dichotomy between social work and the Gospel. He rented four pews in Chicago's Plymouth Congregational Church and filled them with men from Chicago's streets. During his work with the burgeoning Sunday school movement, he met Ira Sankey (1840–1908), whom he enlisted as a song leader in his evangelistic meetings.

In 1873 Moody and Sankey embarked on a two-year preaching tour of Great Britain. Returning to the states as an established evangelist, Moody conducted evangelistic tours of Brooklyn, Philadelphia, New York, Chicago, and Boston from 1875 to 1879. Throughout the eighties and into the nineties, Moody transformed evangelism as he preached throughout the United States and Europe.

D. L. Moody was the focal point for urban revival in America and Europe. His preaching style and organizational skills brought a new level of refinement to revivalism. As a businessman, his managerial techniques appealed to the growing middle class of industrial America. The business community avidly supported his campaigns and gave his meetings a middle class flavor. His preaching was simple, pleasant, and straightforward—setting forth ruin by sin, redemption by Christ, and regeneration by the Holy Spirit. He laced his sermons with stories that cut to the heart of America's struggles with the loss of agricultural simplicity and the pressures of industrial, urban civilization. He traveled over a million miles and preached to more than 100 million people.

Moody not only transformed evangelism, but he also left an important institutional legacy. Believing that education was foundational for Christianity, he established two schools—Northfield Seminary for girls and Mount Hermon School for boys. In addition, in 1886 he established the Chicago Evangelization Society, later known as Moody Bible Institute. Finally, he started the Northfield summer Bible Conference in 1880, a forerunner of the Bible conference movement that swept across late-nineteenth-century America.

BILLY SUNDAY

Moody's successor in the development of mass evangelism was William (Billy) Ashley Sunday (1862–1935). Born near Ames, Iowa, Sunday at first pursued a baseball career; but in 1886 he was converted to Christ at Chicago's Pacific Garden Mission. In 1891 he walked away from baseball to become a full-time minister, first with the YMCA and then with J. Wilbur Chapman (1859–1918), another pioneer in mass evangelism. But after 1896, Sunday was on his own.

At first his emphasis was on small Midwestern towns, but gradually by 1915 larger cities all over America held Billy Sunday crusades. The hallmark of his urban crusades was the huge wooden tabernacle. Sunday's preaching style, which included colorful, bombastic antics and well-planned theatrics, gained him fame and attention. In addition, the Sunday crusades were a genius of organization. Before each crusade, an advance team of at least twenty specialists descended on the town arranging publicity, music, and business support. The team recruited thousands of church volunteers. At the center of such strategic planning was Sunday's wife, Helen Amelia Thompson.

Sunday's simple message reached over 100 million people, with about one million converts. But his influence extended far beyond conversions. He stood undaunted against alcohol use. In fact, he bears significant responsibility for the passage of the Prohibition Amendment to the U. S. Constitution. He likewise championed patriotism during World War I, arguing that "Christianity and patriotism are synonyms" and that "hell and traitors are synonyms" (Noll, 115-119). He helped raise millions of dollars for the military effort. Few Christian leaders have ever had a more significant impact on shaping American culture.

BILLY GRAHAM

Present-day evangelism and revivalism centers on Billy Graham (b. 1918). Born in North Carolina, Graham evidenced preaching skills even at an early age. After ordination as a Southern Baptist preacher and a brief pastorate, Graham became the first full-time employee of Youth for Christ in 1944. Graham's 1949 twelve-week Los Angeles crusade was a watershed in modern evangelism. Athletes, mobsters, and Hollywood stars professed faith in Christ. National attention resulted. Therefore, in 1950, Graham organized the Billy Graham Evangelistic Association and the *Hour of Decision* radio program. His 1954 crusade in England gained him international acclaim.

Billy Graham's message was the same as that of other evangelists, but his style differed. At first his hatred of communism mixed a forceful patriotism with the gospel message. He even befriended presidents such as Truman and Nixon. But Nixon's resignation caused Graham to back away from the perception of partisan politics. Graham's 1959 New York crusade marked the other determinative characteristics of his style. He included representatives of mainline Protestant churches in planning the crusade, causing many of the more conservative Protestants to label him a liberal. Graham also integrated African-Americans into his ministry and crusades and achieved the support of Roman Catholics as well. Finally, he penetrated Communist countries with the Gospel several years before the collapse of communism in Europe. He has also visited Communist China and North Korea, preaching and meeting with prominent Communist leaders.

In an age of few heroes, Graham has been a sterling example of integrity. Rarely responding to criticism, he has remained focused on proclaiming the Gospel. His use of technology has allowed him to preach to more people than any other individual in history. Arguably, he stands out as the evangelical statesman of the twentieth century.

Revivalism and evangelism in this century are a far cry from similar movements of colonial America. Theology seems less important to the twenty-first-century evangelist than it did to Jonathan Edwards in the eighteenth century. Perhaps the emphasis on method and technology has cost the church much when it comes to theological maturity and discipleship. Is the modern church stressing "just believe" and ignoring the importance of doctrine? This question is difficult to answer. But it reflects one of the central issues of today—the struggle of the church with modernity.

FOR FURTHER DISCUSSION

1. Summarize the three phases of the First Great Awakening.
2. Show why Jonathan Edwards and George Whitefield were so important to the Awakening.
3. Discuss several effects of the First Awakening.
4. How were the First and Second Awakenings different?
5. What was the Layman's Prayer Revival of 1858?
6. What is mass evangelism? How did D. L. Moody and Billy Sunday influence its development?
7. How did Billy Graham influence the development of evangelism in the modern age?

What If Edward Kimball Had Not Told a Shoe Clerk in Boston About Christ?

If Sunday school teacher Edward Kimball had not been faithful to share his faith with a Boston shoe clerk, the world might not have heard about Dwight L. Moody, Billy Sunday, or Billy Graham. But Kimball was faithful, and in 1856 Dwight L. Moody came to faith in Christ, and the world has never been the same. God called Moody into evangelism, and in 1879 while he was preaching in England, an evangelistic fervor was awakened in the heart of Frederick B. Meyer, the pastor of a small church.

Years later while Meyer was preaching on an American college campus, a student named J. Wilbur Chapman professed faith in Christ. Chapman went on to hold evangelistic meetings across America. He later hired a new convert (and former major league baseball player), Billy Sunday, to work as an advance man in his ministry. In a few years Chapman went into the pastorate, and Sunday began to lead his own evangelistic crusades.

In 1924 Billy Sunday held a crusade in Charlotte, North Carolina. After the meetings about thirty men formed the Charlotte Men's Club, which met on a regular basis for prayer. Ten years later the club met for a day of prayer and fasting in a grove of trees at Frank Graham's dairy farm. The main focus of the day was to prepare for an upcoming crusade to be held in Charlotte. One of the men, Vernon Patterson, prayed that "out of Charlotte the Lord would raise up someone to preach the Gospel to the ends of the earth." Patterson had no idea that the answer to his prayer was a few hundred yards away, pitching hay into feeding troughs. During the crusade led by Mordecai Ham, Frank Graham's son Billy committed his life to Christ.

Because Edward Kimball was faithful, the world has been blessed by the ministries of Dwight L. Moody, J. Wilbur Chapman, Billy Sunday, Mordecai Ham, Billy Graham, and thousands of other men and women the world has never heard of, like Vernon Patterson. Church history is in large part a record of the faithfulness of people like Edward Kimball and Vernon Patterson.

Based on information from the *Encyclopedia of 7,700 Illustrations: Signs of the Times,* Paul Lee Tan, ed. (Rockville, Md.: Assurance Publishers, 1979) and *A Prophet with Honor: The Billy Graham Story* by William Martin (New York: William Morrow, 1991).

THE CHURCH AND MODERNITY

What is the relation between Christianity and modern culture;
may Christianity be maintained in a scientific age?

J. GRESHAM MACHEN,

CHRISTIANITY AND LIBERALISM, 1923

The modern world has not been kind to the church. As earlier chapters have shown, the antisupernaturalism of the Enlightenment had devastating results for theology and by the twentieth century had filtered down to the ordinary church member, especially in the mainline denominations. The term "modernity" involves accommodating Christian theology to antisupernaturalism. So modernity asks: Is the Bible really the Word of God? Can the church really trust the first three chapters of Genesis? Are science and the Bible friends or enemies? What exactly is salvation, and how is it defined?

THE SOURCES OF MODERNITY

Before Charles Darwin (1809-1882), most people in Western civilization believed that the design they observed in the physical world proved the existence of God and that everything had a fixed order or place. Each species was separately created by God, and each had a specific purpose in the mind of God. Darwin's 1859 publication of *Origin of Species* shattered these assumptions for many. Those who accepted Darwin's theory thought that he had undermined the authority of Scripture, especially in terms of Creation. Darwin argued that a struggle for existence characterized the natural world, resulting in all organic beings adapting to the changing dynamics of their environment. Thus, by natural selection unfavorable variations and those possessing them are eliminated. He thought that this process of natural selection over vast periods of time explains how different species evolve.

Darwin's theory of evolution had catastrophic effects for Christianity. First, it questioned the literal interpretation of the Bible, especially of Genesis 1. Does "day" mean a twenty-four-hour day? Natural selection also argued against a special Creation of God as recorded in Genesis. Doubt about the Bible's authority resulted. Second, natural selection removed the idea of purpose and design from nature. Chance was now seen as the powerful force controlling natural selection. People now thought that the intricacy and interconnectedness of nature did not necessarily demonstrate the handiwork of God. Third, the idea of order and fixity in nature was questioned. For Darwin, nature was in a state of flux and change via natural selection; the word was change, not permanence. Fourth, Darwin's hypothesis was destructive to the idea of the uniqueness of man, so central to Christian theology. For Darwin, man was a product of time and chance. Key doctrines, such as the image of God in humankind, the entrance of sin into the race by the Fall, and the need for a Savior, were all brought into question. Darwin shook Christianity at its very foundation.

A second source of modernity was the social gospel. With the rise of industrial capitalism came massive social problems—vast urban industrial centers teeming with workers who lived in slums. These urban centers festered with dirt, exploitation, crime, and poverty. In addition, immigrants of different ethnic, racial, and religious backgrounds flowed into the cities where child labor predominated. Christian leaders, therefore, asked what the role of the Gospel was in those conditions. Could Christianity and socialism be reconciled? What was the social dimension of Christianity? As Christians struggled with these questions, a response known as the social gospel emerged.

The social gospel was liberal Christianity's response to the crisis of modern industrialism. Men like Walter Rauschenbush (1861–1918) and Washington Gladden (1836–1918) theologically revised the Gospel. Sin was defined as corporate and environmental, not individual and inborn. The problems of humanity were caused by the conditions of society, they said, not by the sin nature of each individual. Therefore, salvation was redefined to involve changing a person's surroundings, helping to organize labor unions, and working for legislation to improve human conditions. The social gospel defined sin and salvation as external, with no real emphasis given to the internal corruption of humanity.

The third source of modernity centered on further undermining of the Bible's authority. Coming from Germany, a movement called higher criticism questioned the authorship of biblical books, as well as the traditionally accepted dates and purposes for the biblical texts. German scholars doubted Mosaic authorship of the Pentateuch, for example. Julius Wellhausen (1844–1918) argued that these books were really written by four unknown authors (he identified them by the letters J, D, E, P), not Moses. In New Testament criticism, F. C. Baur (1792–1860) asserted that Paul wrote only Romans, Galatians, and the Corinthian letters. In addition, Baur placed all four Gospels in the second half of the second century. These critics questioned the authority of God's Word, saying it could not be trusted.

Because many of the Protestant scholars in America studied in Europe or used European scholarly texts, Darwinism, the social gospel, and higher critical thinking became a part of seminary education in America. By the opening of the twentieth century, most of these ideas were common in mainline Protestantism. Pastors taking the pulpits in America reflected these ideas, and their preaching and counseling likewise exhibited a commitment to what was then called "modernism."

FIGHT FOR CONTROL OF THE DENOMINATIONS

Between 1910 and 1930, among the largest of the Protestant denominations—Northern Baptists, Northern Presbyterians, and Northern Methodists—a struggle for control ensued between the fundamentalists and the modernists. On the surface, issues such as administration of foreign missions and control of denominational magazines defined the conflict. However, the real concern centered on theology. The modernist wing of Protestantism had abandoned the inerrancy of Scripture, the Virgin Birth, the deity of Christ, His Second Coming, and His substitutionary atonement. The fundamentalists, through writing, preaching, and teaching, defended adherence to these fundamental doctrines as central to Christianity. In every major case, the fundamentalists lost control of the denominations.

The successes of nineteenth-century revivalism had lulled fundamentalism into complacency. The Bible conference movement, begun in the 1870s and 1880s, often separated those committed to historic

Christian orthodoxy from the mainline churches. In addition, the Bible institute movement, begun in the same time period, provided practical, abbreviated, and efficient biblical education to laypeople. These schools trained missionaries and gave extraordinary opportunities to women, but they also reinforced the separatism taking place. The preaching ministries of Moody and Sunday widened the chasm between fundamentalists and modernists. Publications such as *The Scofield Reference Bible* (1907) and *The Fundamentals* (1910) defined the theological issues of the struggle.

With control lost, what did the fundamentalists do? First, many formed new denominational groups. The Presbyterians formed the Orthodox Presbyterian Church, the Bible Presbyterian Church, and the Reformed Presbyterian Church. Some Baptists formed the General Association of Regular Baptist Churches, the Conservative Baptist Association, and the Baptist Bible Fellowship. In addition, the numbers of independent churches exploded across America. Second, conservative fundamentalists formed interdenominational groups such as the Independent Fundamental Churches of America (1930) and the National Association of Evangelicals (1942) that worked together to promote conservative theological causes.

The formation of parachurch ministries was a third response of the conservatives. Ministries founded for youth work, such as Word of Life (1941), Young Life (1941), and Youth for Christ (1944), were designed to reach a whole generation of young people. College ministries—InterVarsity Christian Fellowship of America (1941) and Campus Crusade for Christ (1951)—represented concerted efforts to reach the universities. Evangelical Teacher Training Association (1930) was started to help standardize and develop a curriculum to train Bible teachers in colleges, Bible institutes, and local churches. The radio became a powerful teaching tool through the ministries of *The Old Fashioned Revival Hour* of Charles Fuller, *Back to the Bible* of Theodore Epp, and *Radio Bible Class* of M. R. DeHaan.

THE FRAGMENTATION OF CONSERVATIVE PROTESTANTISM

By the 1950s, fundamentalist Protestantism was rife with tension. In the judgment of many conservative Christians, the fundamentalist-modernist controversy of the twenties and thirties had left the fundamentalists bruised, defensive, suspicious, and increasingly separatistic. Therefore, a group of conservative Christians, later known as neo-evangelicals and led by Harold John Ockenga (1905–1985), broke with fundamentalism. Together with Billy Graham and Carl Henry (b. 1913), Ockenga sought to reform fundamentalism to be more scholarly and to put more emphasis on apologetics and the social dimension of Christianity. They founded Fuller Theological Seminary in California to champion this reform. Christianity Today, a magazine founded by Billy Graham and his father-in-law, L. Nelson Bell, in 1955, was considered the unofficial voice of the movement.

Over issues such as the inerrancy of Scripture, questions about eschatology, and the role of the social sciences in meeting people's needs, a further fragmentation of conservative Christianity occurred in the 1970s and 1980s. A younger generation of evangelicals, represented in publications such as The Wittenberg Door and Sojourners magazine, argued that neo-evangelicalism did not go far enough. As political and social activists, these evangelicals, led by individuals such as Ron Sider and Tony Campolo, pressed the church to consider its social responsibility and to give less emphasis to theological questions. The result is that today conservative, evangelical, fundamentalist Christianity is increasingly divided.

Further fragmentation of Protestantism is evident in the explosion of "renewal" movements in the twentieth century. Originating in the early years of the century, Pentecostalism challenged Protestants to think about the issues of sanctification and the Holy Spirit in a new way. Proclaiming the connection between baptism of the Holy Spirit and speaking in tongues, the Azusa Street Revival in Los Angeles (1906) spread throughout the world and eventually led to the formation of several new denominational groups such as the Assemblies of God, the Church of God (Cleveland, Tenn.), the Church of God of Prophecy, and the Church of God in Christ. Over time the Pentecostal movement gained respectability and legitimacy as these denominations experienced rapid growth in the United States and overseas. But the mainline denominations were largely left untouched by Pentecostalism.

In the late 1950s and into the 1960s, groups such as those led by businessman Demos Shakarian (1913–1993) and Pentecostal preacher Oral Roberts (b. 1918) committed themselves to penetrating the mainline churches with what came to be known as the charismatic renewal. To model that goal, Roberts joined the United Methodist Church in 1968. Throughout the 1960s and 1970s, charismatic renewal groups formed in every major denomination—Methodist, Presbyterian, Lutheran, Episcopalian, and the Roman Catholic Church. The charismatic movement emphasized not only the gift of tongues, but also words of knowledge and prophecy as well as faith healings. Nationwide conferences throughout this period demonstrated that what united the various renewal movements was more a shared experience of the Spirit than theology.

In the 1980s, a "third wave" of renewal spread across the church, heralded by individuals like John Wimber (1931–1997) and Fuller Seminary professor C. Peter Wagner (b. 1930). The third wave movement identified "the signs and wonders" of the New Testament book of Acts as legitimate demonstrations of God's power today. These signs were seen as authenticating Christ's ambassadors. Hence, proponents speak of "power evangelism" and "power encounters" that prove God's existence and validate the gospel message. The "Signs and Wonders" movement expressly appeals to evangelicals who have traditionally rejected such demonstrations of power as appropriate only for the first century. The most significant example of this was the embrace of the third wave by former Dallas Theological Seminary professor Jack Deere.

THE GROWTH OF THE BLACK CHURCH

The Black church in America had its origins in the slave religion of the American South. Deprived of their identity, oppressed by their masters, and unable to establish their own institutions, many slaves turned to Christianity. Faith in Jesus Christ gave them hope for the future when His justice would right the wrongs done to them. Negro spirituals embodied the vibrant faith of a subjugated people who looked to God for justice and mercy.

The Black church began to organize into denominations quite early in the national period. The African Methodist Episcopal Zion Church was formed in 1816 with Richard Allen (a former slave) as its first bishop. The National Baptist Convention of the USA, formed in 1915, was an amalgamation of three Baptist groups that today, after additional mergers, has a membership in excess of 6.5 million members. Many Pentecostal groups also formed during the twentieth century. One of the fastest growing churches in America and the fifth largest denomination is the Church of God in Christ (COGIC). Founded by Charles Harrison Mason in 1897, the church adopted its Pentecostal distinctives and its current name in 1907. Currently with membership of over 6.75 million, COGIC churches grew more than 48 percent between 1982 and 1991.

The modern civil rights movement largely grew out of the Black church. Leaders such as Dr. Martin Luther King, Jr., were themselves Baptist preachers who believed that the Bible condemned discrimination and racism. King, the undisputed leader of the nonviolent civil rights movement, organized African-Americans and whites to pursue justice for all Americans regardless of race. Using the Bible and nonviolence, the movement impacted all aspects of American society.

ROMAN CATHOLICISM AND MODERNITY

The modern world has not been kind to Roman Catholicism either. In fact, the twentieth century witnessed a crisis of authority in Catholicism. During the nineteenth century, the Roman Catholic Church (RCC) attempted to consolidate its authority through a series of decisive declarations aimed at defining doctrine and papal power. In 1854 the RCC declared the immaculate conception of Mary. Through the merits of Jesus, the RCC pronounced that Mary was preserved from the effects of original sin and therefore sinless. In 1869 it issued the Syllabus of Errors, which announced that when the Pope spoke *ex cathedra* (from his chair), he was speaking infallibly. Finally, Vatican Council I (1869–1870) affirmed papal infallibility. The papacy utilized this power only once, in 1950, when Pope Pius XII proclaimed the dogma of Mary's bodily assumption into heaven.

During the twentieth century, Roman Catholicism experienced its greatest struggles since the Reformation. Largely through Vatican Council II (1963–1965), the RCC answered the challenges of modernism. In the documents that resulted from the council, the RCC embraced the ecumenical movement. The RCC has thus been in dialogue with various Protestant denominations and the Eastern Orthodox Church. Vatican II likewise avowed papal infallibility and the equality of Scripture and church tradition as sources of authority for Catholics. However, it was in the practical areas that Vatican II had its most revolutionary impact. The council made optional some traditional expressions of Catholicism—Latin in the liturgy, meatless Fridays, Lenten fasts and abstinence, the cult of the saints, and the regular practice of confession to the priests. Vatican II thus removed many of the cultural distinctives of Catholicism.

Today the Roman Catholic Church under Pope John Paul II is struggling with how to respond to liberation theology in Latin America, the charismatic movement in western Europe and America, pressures to allow the ordination of women into the priesthood, and ethical questions such as abortion, contraception, euthanasia, and divorce. The RCC has officially taken strong stands on each of these questions, but many Catholics reject the official position, thereby heightening the crisis of authority.

The modern world has brought profound challenges to the church of Jesus Christ. This chapter has highlighted some of those challenges and reviewed how the church responded. The twenty-first-century world is one of continuous and permeating change. One thing that can be learned from history is that the church needs to remember its mission and its Head. With that focus, the church will not lose its way and will remain the instrument God uses to bring people to Himself in salvation.

FOR FURTHER DISCUSSION

1. Summarize how each of the following contributed to modernity and challenged the church:
   Darwinism—
   Social gospel—
   German higher criticism—
2. What was the fundamentalist-modernist controversy in the American denominations? Who won the struggle?
3. List some of the responses of fundamentalists to the loss of control of the major denominations.
4. Summarize the differences between Pentecostalism, the charismatic movement, and the "Signs and Wonders" movement.
5. What is the difference between a fundamentalist and an evangelical?
6. Summarize the developments in Roman Catholicism in the last century.

NOTES

8 THE CHURCH AND THE SCIENTIFIC REVOLUTION

1. Butt, John, ed. *The Poems of Alexander Pope* (New Haven, Conn.: Yale University Press, 1963), p. 808.

10 THE CHURCH AND MODERN MISSIONS

1. For more information on the history of missions, see Hulbert, Terry C., and Mulholland, Kenneth E., *World Missions Today* (Wheaton, Ill.: Evangelical Training Association, 1990).

11 THE CHURCH AND REVIVALS IN AMERICA

1. "New measures" was a phrase used by critics of Finney in the 1820s. See Mark Noll, *History of Christianity in the United States and Canada* (Grand Rapids: Wm. B. Eerdmans Publishing Co., 1992), p. 175.

GLOSSARY

Apology—When used as a theological term, it refers to making a defense of what is held to be true. Apologetics has to do with the study of evidences from Scripture and nature used to present a logical defense of the truth of Christianity.

Bishop—From the Greek word *episkopos* (ep-is'-kop-os), it means "overseer." In early church history, a bishop was a minister who was responsible for the oversight of several churches.

Catechetical School—Catechetical comes from the Greek word *katecheo* (kat-ay-kheh'-o), which means to "teach" or to "instruct." The Catechetical Schools in the early church followed the Socratic approach of teaching, which utilized a question-and-answer methodology.

Church—From the Greek word *ekklesia* (ek-klay-see'-ah), it means "called out ones" or simply "assembly." In reference to the Christian church, *church* has two meanings. The first is the universal or invisible church, which is made up of all born-again believers in Jesus Christ. The second usage (most prevalent in this book) is used to refer to the visible, organized church, which is made up of both believers and unbelievers.

Circa—When used with a date, it means "approximately," indicating uncertainty about the ability of historians to pinpoint it with absolute precision.

Diet of Worms—The formal assembly of German princes that had legislative authority. Martin Luther was tried before this body in 1521 in the German city of Worms.

Emasculate the Gospel—To remove the very heart from the gospel message of salvation and thus make it ineffective.

Erudition—Refers to extensive knowledge, usually gained from the study of books.

Free-grace Gospel—The good news of salvation based fully on the unmerited favor of God being bestowed upon believers through no self-generated activity.

Monasticism—An approach to life that calls for physical isolation from the world and usually is accompanied by the taking of vows such as chastity and poverty. Monasticism is characterized by an emphasis on obedience and authority as well as a desire for seclusion, order, and routine.

Veneration—Means to "worship." Often used by the Roman Catholic Church as in the "veneration of Mary" or the "veneration of the saints."

BIBLIOGRAPHY

CHAPTER 1

Bruce, F. F. *New Testament History*. New York: Anchor, 1972.

Cairns, Earle E. *Christianity Through the Centuries*. Grand Rapids: Zondervan, 1981.

Foh, Susan. *Women and the Word of God*. Philadelphia: Presbyterian and Reformed, 1979.

Hoehner, Harold. *Chronological Aspects of the Life of Christ*. Grand Rapids: Zondervan, 1977.

CHAPTER 2

Lightfoot, J. B. *The Apostolic Fathers*. Grand Rapids: Baker, 1978.

CHAPTER 3

Frend, W. H. C. *The Early Church*. Philadelphia: Lippincott, 1966.

Gonzalez, Justo L. *A History of Christian Thought*, Vol. 1. Nashville: Abingdon, 1970.

CHAPTER 4

Brown, Peter. *Augustine of Hippo*. Berkeley: University of California Press, 1967.

Kelly, J. N. D. *Early Christian Doctrines*. New York: Harper and Row, 1978.

Leith, John H., ed. *Creeds of the Churches*. Atlanta: John Knox Press, 1982.

CHAPTER 5

Gonzalez, Justo L. *A History of Christian Thought*, Vol. 2. Nashville: Abingdon, 1971.

Southern, R. W. *Western Society and the Church in the Middle Ages*. New York: Penguin, 1970.

CHAPTER 6

Bainton, Roland H. *Here I Stand: A Life of Martin Luther.* New York: Abingdon, 1950.

_____. *The Reformation of the Sixteenth Century.* Boston: Beacon, 1952.

Schaff, Phillip. *History of the Christian Church.* New York: Charles Scribner and Co., 1871.

Spitz, Lewis W. *The Protestant Reformation, 1517-1559.* New York: Harper, 1985.

CHAPTER 7

Gonzalez, Justo L. *A History of Christian Thought*, Vol. 2. Nashville: Abingdon, 1971.

Olin, John C. *The Catholic Reformation.* New York: Harper, 1969.

CHAPTER 8

Deason, G. B. "The Protestant Reformation and the Rise of Modern Science." *Scottish Journal of Theology* 38:221-40.

Gonzalez, Justo L. *The Story of Christianity: The Reformation to the Present Day.* New York: Harper, 1984.

Hall, A. R. *The Scientific Revolution, 1500-1800.* Boston: Beacon, 1962.

CHAPTER 9

Fletcher, William C. *The Moderns: Molders of Contemporary Theology.* Grand Rapids: Zondervan, 1962.

Gay, Peter. *The Enlightenment: An Interpretation.* New York: Knopf, 1966-69.

Geisler, Norman. *Christian Apologetics.* Grand Rapids: Baker, 1976.

Gonzalez, Justo L. *A History of Christian Thought*, Vol. 3. Nashville: Abingdon, 1975.

McGrath, Alister E. *The Making of Modern German Christology: 1750-1990.* Grand Rapids: Zondervan, 1994.

Redman, Ben Ray, ed. *The Portable Voltaire.* New York: Viking, 1949, 1963.

Ritschl, Albrecht. *The Christian Doctrine of Justification and Reconciliation.* Clifton, N.J.: Reference Book Publishers, 1996.

Chapter 10

Latourette, Kenneth Scott. *A History of the Expansion of Christianity*. New York: Harper, 1941-1944.

Chapter 11

Murray, Iain. *Revival and Revivalism: The Making and Marring of American Evangelicalism, 1750-1858*. Carlisle, Pa.: Banner of Truth, 1994.

Noll, Mark A. *A History of Christianity in the United States and Canada*. Grand Rapids: Eerdmans, 1992.

Smith, Timothy L. *Revivalism and Social Reform: American Protestantism on the Eve of the Civil War*. Gloucester: Peter Smith, 1976.

Weisberger, Bernard A. *They Gathered at the River: The Story of the Great Revivalists and Their Impact Upon Religion in America*. Chicago: Quadrangle, 1966.

Chapter 12

Noll, Mark. *A History of Christianity in the United States and Canada*. Grand Rapids: Eerdmans, 1992.

Since 1930
Evangelical Training Association

THE MINISTRIES OF EVANGELICAL TRAINING ASSOCIATION (ETA)

Experienced – Founded in 1930.
Doctrinally Dependable – Conservative and evangelical theology.
Educationally Sound – Engaging all adult learning styles.
Thoroughly Field-Tested – Used by a global constituency.
Recommended – Officially endorsed by denominations and schools.
Ministry Driven – Committed to quality training resources for equipping lay volunteers to serve Christ more effectively in the church.
Affordable – Attractive and reasonably priced.

For many local ministries, the most important step to an effective lay leadership training program is locating and implementing an inspiring, motivational system of instruction. ETA curriculum is available as traditional classroom courses, audio and video seminars, audio and video CD-ROM packages, and other resources for your classroom teaching or personal study.

Contact ETA today for free information and a 20-minute video presentation. Request Information Packet: Crossway Partner.

EVANGELICAL TRAINING ASSOCIATION
110 Bridge Street • PO Box 327 • Wheaton, IL 60189
800-369-8291 • FAX 630-668-8437 • www.etaworld.org

PERSONAL NOTES

PERSONAL NOTES

PERSONAL NOTES

PERSONAL NOTES